A Victorian Dollhousing Ceremony

a poetic opera

Kristin Garth,
Tianna G. Hansen,
& Justin Karcher

Rhythm & Bones Press
Trauma-turned-Art

Rhythm & Bones Press
Birdsboro, Pennsylvania

Interior Design: Tianna G. Hansen, *Rhythm & Bones Press*
Cover Design: Tianna G. Hansen
Illustrations by: Russ Daum
ISBN: 978-0-9980432-6-5
Printed by *Ingram Spark, Inc.,* USA
First Edition June 2019

www.rhythmnbone.com/avdc

"*A Victorian Dollhousing Ceremony* is written by a trifecta of talented poets who have created an intriguing, original work. This is a stunning fever dream, set in an urban wasteland full of boozy magic-drenched parties and sociopaths who are able to use magic to make the world a much worse place than it already is. It's about female rivalry. It's about male desire to possess. It's about the perception of perfection, as well as the effects of trauma. I've never read anything quite like it, but it's positively spellbinding."

~ Jessica Drake-Thomas

A Note to Our Readers

We thank each and every one of you for claiming a copy of this special collaboration and invite you to join us in our poetic opera, *A Victorian Dollhousing Ceremony*. The premise of this book began as a nightmare that Kristin had one evening about being shrunken down and 'dollhoused' – and as she fittingly put it the other day, we have never been more grateful for a nightmare before. That is what brought you this beautiful book today. Kristin recruited Justin and Tianna to play the roles in this opera, a dark and enchanting tale about becoming reborn and discovering self-love as a source of appreciation and acceptance; about a dying wizard as he grapples with the humanity (or lack thereof) that surrounds him. This tale looks in the face of evil - of villains, rivals, frenemies, captors and captives. It begins with the birth of each of our characters, THE WIZARD (Justin Karcher), who is the book's villain (or anti-hero), THE DOLL (Kristin Garth), captivated with dollhouses, and THE FIREBIRD (Tianna G. Hansen), a dancer consumed by a love for fire and a burning desire for attention and recognition. THE DOLL lives inside both a mundane and magical society where wizards are whispers you might wander into one night. So, we welcome you to join us in this world. Allow THE WIZARD to whisper in your ear and become enchanted.

This is, ultimately, a work of fantasy but each character holds a deeper part of the author who wrote them. A word of caution: this tale is not for the faint hearted and deals with many difficult subjects, including sexual assault, abuse, and child abuse. We ask that you tread with this tale lightly, and should you find it too difficult to continue, please step back. We are overjoyed if you are able to continue on with us, and please remember this is a fantasy world you are about to enter. We hope you can find the liberation that we all did while composing this operatic tale through poetry.

~ Justin Karcher (The Wizard),
Kristin Garth (The Doll), and
Tianna G. Hansen (The Firebird)

A Victorian Dollhousing Ceremony

"I must stand quite alone,
if I am to understand myself
and everything about me."

–

HENRIK IBSEN
A Doll's House

The Ceremonies

i.

Birth

a Wizard,
a Doll,
&
a Firebird

A Wizard is Born Outside a Mighty City

THE WIZARD (Justin Karcher)

Before my teeth were swampy gemstones, I was but a boy
begging for scraps on the outskirts of some walled city
here was the mighty city with its musclemen and gutter nuns
here was the mighty city with its garbage trucks and concert halls
the songs the police sing when they beat desert into rain
what firefighters sing as they shove candles into graves
here was the mighty city mangling widows with debt and cobblestone
here was the mighty city shattering windows with bathtub bones
here were glittering streets lined with hollow cars and wedding cakes
here were cemeteries disguised as condos where parents went missing
here was the mighty city disguised as a childless chariot going nowhere
here was the mighty city with its toilet paper and rooftops pissing
here were flesh dungeons disguised as preschools crying everywhere
here was the mighty city that threw out orphans like me, away from fake light
into the asphalt waste where we chewed on deaf dandelions
that never heard our cries
begging whatever to give us flowers and not weeds, anything but impossible seeds
we would build giant beds out of animal fur and trampoline guts but never fall asleep
bouncing up and down toward the snores of stars never awake to give us our dreams
here was the mighty city that would send out planes
dropping lawnmowers and Red Bull
here were the orphans sticking their fingers into the machinery and praying for wings
death was everywhere back then, we were cast out like autumn leaves
cast out when chill burns out the roots, we had no trees that branched us into air
so we untangled kites from bug hair and dreamed up a wind that looked like home
searching for the words that could swerve chaos into health
ground without the shakes
here was the modern age, but all the calendars were fakes
and all the clocks secondhand
so time moved like broken men, sluggish from sunrise to sunset
then they dropped like flies
we were the orphans that turned maggots into magic
scissors to the sky and never look back

Dark Leaves

THE DOLL (Kristin Garth)

Her love's embrace is gnarled & deep, shadow
tentacled, cloaks girl grief beneath. A weep
to sleep against his mottled trunk, she knows
this path red wine stumble drunk. Grey sheep
black hooves, dire bleats with fangs, blue tongues
fly-stung-infected brains. A flock inside
subconscious rot, her nightmarescape dreamed young,
forgot. He was her cradle, sometimes slide,
skinned knees, chemise, scaled bark to hide an hour,
an afternoon — her shut eye secrets bud
a bloom blood moon as Pinot devoured
the decades post deflowering. A flood
of memories drowned in wine, found in leaves,
his lullabies familiarly diseased.

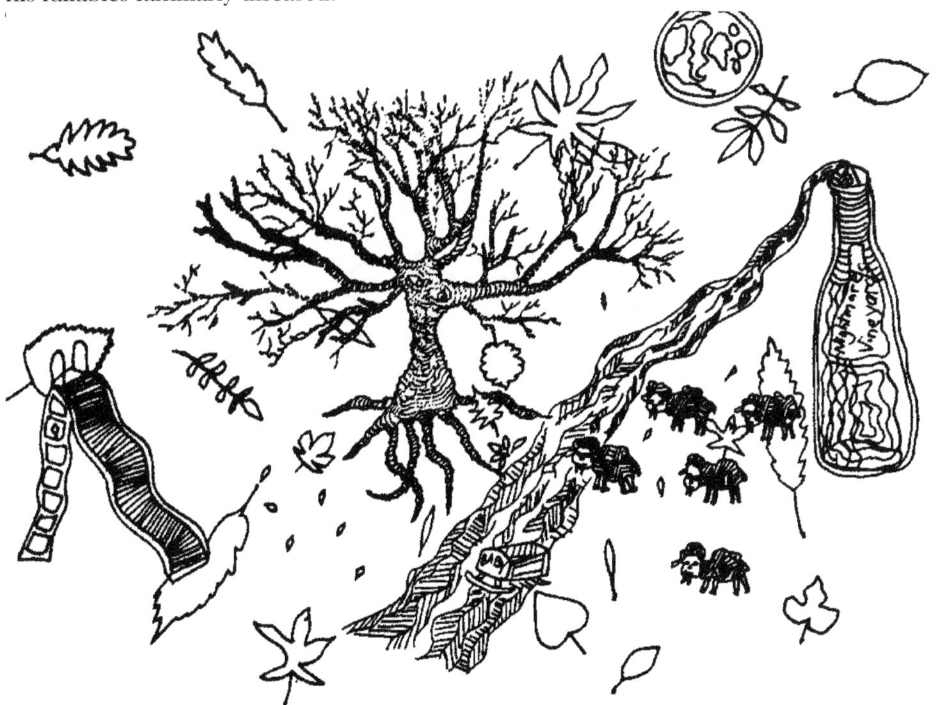

Dancer, Delicate

THE FIREBIRD (Tianna G. Hansen)

Always wanted to be a dancer
elegant, toes pointed like roots
to grow deep through soil
feeling them sinking deeper

always wanted to feel like flying
across the stage, above an audience
captivated by your beauty
your mother said *you'll never be
a dancer*, you'll never grow wings

that was before, before you silenced her
now she's captive in your glance
captive in how you breathe
how you soar across the stage
she is in every breath of you
every movement, perfected
each tilt and twirl and bend

you feel her beneath you, reaching
like she still wants to grip these roots
sprawling beyond even her now

you are a dancer, delicate
more than you ever dreamed.

ii.

Pangs

The Firefighter's Daughter

THE DOLL

He'll tell you a story to save your life:
(firefighter father who frames it as love)
skin pulled from bones of addict or housewife,
dead flesh soils, same, the palms, gold pigskin gloves.

He will show fire gloves charred black by cooked skin
from bodies baked inside bedsheets who thought
a candle romantic; flickers were friends —
unlovable children nobody taught

the way he teaches you terror, preschool
nightmares, flame fraught. Fifth grade, read library books.
about death at the stake, you're certain you'll
perish this way — sin, some mistake. He took

your world beneath covers, burned his child-wife.
He told you a story to save your life.

Pirouette

THE FIREBIRD

His hands moved you like strings
attached to a marionette deftly,
as you danced for him your body lifted
to each movement of his hands like
a caress along every inch.
you would feel him as you swung into a
perfect pirouette, you the lithe tigress
stalking in the high grass and he
your Master. Bring to him your prey;
audience's applause is what he craves
you are nothing but a living doll, weep
in the dead of night alone in bed
cradling broken and bloody feet
imagining him beside you, tracing
your outline - curves lost to a habit,
a passion of dance, twisting your body
in his fingers. deep sighs of desire
what you will never possess but oh,
how you wish for deft strokes on bare skin,
to come alive for him between the sheets
as you do on polished floor, pristine form
cut to his every desire - he tells you higher,
you leap; he tells you lower, you dive...
you would break your bones to conform
    - anything for him.

the pangs of your heart are plastered in pink plastic

THE DOLL

five-year-old tears, a purple leo, pink
elastic sewn in painted shoes the night
before the show. a fozzie bear can't think,
stuffed brains, or blink, follows stage right,
your rond de jambe in pastel lights — cute, mute
bystander to your suffering. brown fur,
saliva-matted, buffering disputes
you utter when in bed, cotton murmurs
of childhood, bled, paraded to perform in tights
with animal, wet, hairy smells of men
and your devouring. they will wonder why
you're cowering. you're someplace far from them —
your head between a hand, this cotton bear,
in memories you bring everywhere.

rosebuds

THE FIREBIRD

you were always teacher's pet
                  ((asked you to stay after class))
didn't have anyone to go home to
nobody to eat lunch with or pass
crinkled paper notes, whispers
between the aisles and clasped
hands in the hallways... only
girl you considered friend didn't
want anything to do with you,
                  ((after the midnight escapade))
taken into her room covered in
smoke & guilt lingering, stuck to
your hair and flimsy nightgown.

no family, no friends — outcast
                  ((yet he saw great things in you))
told you how beautiful your eyes
shone, how silky your hair between
fingers. you did not know how to
tell him you didn't like it,   *((any of it.))*
he was the only one who saw you
the only one who felt your worth.
you grew to like it, accept it.

anticipate his fingers locked in
strands of hair, tugging until your
eyes well with tears. Ignore this
screaming pain, become a puppet.
                  ((strings are his to tug)),
move as he pleases. contort into
        any   shape.

wear ribbons in your hair to
catch his eyes, capture notice.
short skirts and long thighs
as you grow, budding breasts

rosebuds peek through cloth
innocence once wrapped you
in a shroud, now stripped away
                    ((naked babe, cold & shivering))
you'll give him anything he pleases.
the cost to see him smile, down on
knees like in prayer, head bowed.
chastity wasn't something you could
afford. never an option for those
who adored you,   ((took everything))
all that's left to call your own
is dance. ballet becomes solace

                    ((always someone you aim to please))

Thirteen

THE DOLL

best ballerina, she will ever be,
pristine routines, victim — puberty bloomed
doom — chest she cannot tape; monstrosities
malign lithe movements, shape. Trades mirrored rooms,

she dyes blonde hair, blue black, eighteen, strip club
peach vintage underwear, velvet, lace trim
six garters, belt. En pointe, takes cash, stage love
above, untouched. You're felt. Women

impugn her nudity. Call you "artist,"
see orchestras, balconies — not dressing rooms, beds,
ignored pleas. Decry sly capitalist's
striptease for chest, flat, cowed, arthritic knees

that bend to célèbre burlesque queens,
you ache to be and pitied at thirteen.

iii.

Flames

Reclaim

THE FIREBIRD

25

flames began   to lick
your skin   to consume you
before you   had the chance
to say   *'no'*   before you knew
you could.

embers trace   a pattern
on your skin   burn
enters bone   become
candlelight   flicker,
coals glow.

you re-ignite   again
              & again
no end to   fire that burns inside
feed off   kindling
anger   oxygen
       pain.

resound, crackle build
resilience   instead of
dying   fire feeds
disgrace   self-hate
power   continues
to grow.

you withstood so much
before the flames came
sole release   moon
shining   perfect orb
greets you   full belly,
beams   of light
on   skin.

fuel   no longer
kindles   ferocity
that will   never die;
one day   flames

ignite   you with joy
rejuvenation   restoration
reclamation   of
soul.

when the flames come
you will   be ready
you will   greet them
with open arms   hands
no longer tied   behind,
bound to   the stake.

entire body   consumed
by scorching   desire
of others placed
upon your   weight.

surviving
thriving
reclaiming
disguise,

phoenix rising
black ashes

                                reborn.

savior saves something to destroy

THE DOLL

a ten-year-old in corduroy, pink tights
hide peacock bruises, older, new, green,
black, purple, yellow hued. trace thin thigh, bright
outline through pink cotton, aquamarine
dance dressing room where you are seen by eyes
ice blue, carried to you, untouchable one
he would rescue, placed her yawning inside
your bed, "my savior," just some dumb
half-conscious thing she said, you can't excise
months later from your head. wet pillow scream
though nothing's said.   resent this spy —
her glimpses, your befouled thighs, mottled cream.
destroyer brought a witness to your grave.
despise this blue-eyed child he chose to save.

Like a Truce

THE FIREBIRD

Backstage blindfolded trust exercise
fall back, he says. *throw your arms to
each side and release* — free fall.
expect to hit the floor, lead ballerina
posed behind you, chocolate eyes,
smirk as she lets you tumble...
but you teeter back, and she meets you
open arms like a truce, catching you.
she lifts you in her arms, this flaming
Phoenix, magnificent, and you feel
as if you could fly. you feel as if you
can soar. admiration from the start
destined for friendship or more,
you turn to her, remove blindfold
and look into her eyes, smiling at this
woman glistening before you.
wrap thin arms around her, whisper
let's call it a truce— trusting
she will catch you again.
pull her to the dressing room
and say,   *can we be friends?*
abusive pasts we now share
secret keepers, confidants,
she extends her arms, an offering.
fold into her breast, feel tears
well into your eyes and you are
again: that little girl, staring up at her,
                             smell of smoke wrapped in hair,
                             adorned in silken charred nightgown
                             wanting nothing more than to find
                             friendship, everlasting. wanting
                                  nothing more than
                                                to find a light
                                         amidst all this darkness.

Choreographers

THE DOLL

By day, you bleed for him, shed big toenail
tear skin, raw opening he'll wiggle in,
your bustle hoop skirt crinoline. Females
a corps descend surround his secret sin.

By night, you bleed within, a sacrifice
that does not end at barre or with your art —
new bruises, uses, love you pay for twice,
pink tights, fishnets, careless rips of heart.

In dreams, you see all of them. His face becomes
a hundred men. First taught you to pretend,
bequeathing punishment with sugarplums.
You bite your lip and let them in again.

Their fingers shape you into what they see.
For them, you suffer this choreography.

iv.

Firebirds

When an Ashtray Turns into a Birdhouse

THE WIZARD

My favorite kind of person is one who chain smokes
therefore my favorite person is an artist struggling with their craft, their voice
because they're always smoking, oh what cancerous evolution
an extra tongue out of the mouth, an extra finger out of the hand
factories suddenly appearing on chapped lips, all that unreal smoke
it's really quite beautiful, pretending cigarettes are wingless birds
that they need to be smoked
to get their wings back, that when you flick a cigarette butt
you're actually pushing a bird
out of a window, whispering, "Now here is where you fly, I'll never kiss you again"

all my life, my body's been like an ashtray of other people's cigarette butts
I would suck up their dreams like a motel pillow, show them a sky full of holes
whisper, "You can fill those holes if you want, just blow, close your eyes and hope"
back then I wanted it all, wanted to untwist the teardrops that fall from our farms
reinvent truths so they don't sound so dull and final, so they land softer on our hearts

I was a fool

I've always been obsessed with the first human who cried, like when did that happen
and where, were they in a cave somewhere, were there screaming animals
and a lonely campfire
still-life scribblings on the rocky wall, was the sun more like a fast flare, here now
gone tomorrow, was darkness more like a hospital, giving birth to monsters that scare
and what of the monsters that drink our worst fears
did they have a choice in any of this?
Sometimes I chain-smoke, pray for cancer, just so I have time to figure out
what I'd miss

I'm still a fool

I remember this one night, me and my friends were partying in a city
that was really a warzone
and the music sounded like the self-mutilation of kings, but also like drum and bass
razorblades flying through charred air toward our wrists, so we touched future's face
thinking this was the end, here are your eyes, your ears, your nose

oh brave new world
we drank everything in sight until we blacked out
real life tweets from the underworld
poems written on lower backs as we bent over words, curved them like horizons
trying to redefine all that we know, we were naked and ready
confused daughter and sons
let's self-destruct, craft a dance floor out of bones and dance real slow into the fog
hold each other until astronomers figure out that there's something more
a different dialogue
so we smoked a million cigarettes, piled them up real high
and our voices were hoarse
so when we tried to scream, nothing but a desert dust
like we were drunk driving a hearse
and that night we tried running from death, for the love of God
just a good night's sleep
bombs practiced gymnastics and jumped over bars
here we were sitting around an ashtray
then suddenly all our cigarette butts started levitating and they swirled together
maybe magic
but they formed a giant firebird, a beast with purpose, wings formed from
why we smoke
it was beautiful and it glided over corpses, hangovers, broken clocks
towards a faraway home

there were times I wasn't so foolish, a dancer on fire and a sky that matters

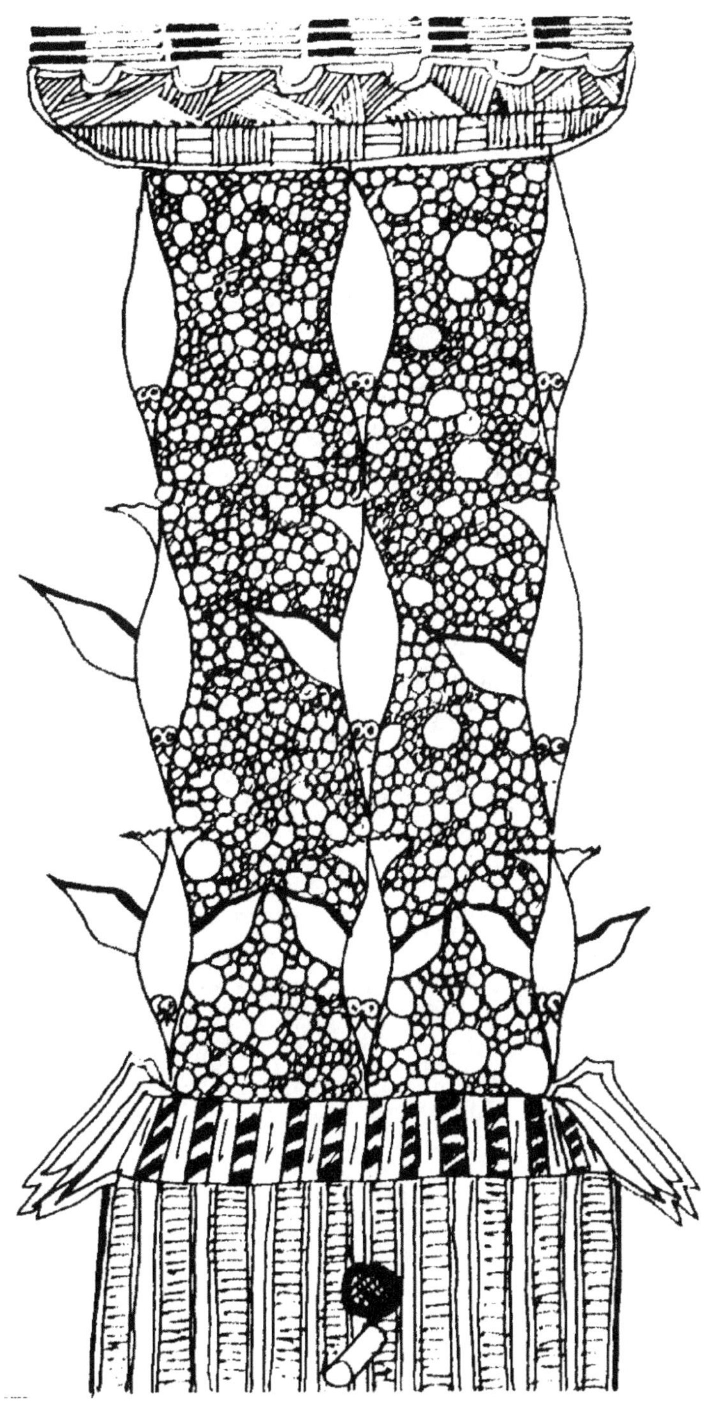

No One Asked You What You Like

THE DOLL

he says, looped satin, slats, midnight, headboard
he ties your wrists too tight. Director, stage,
inside his bed, ribcage he pulls towards
his head, cheek against your shaken heart, rage,
European pink ribbons, private parts.
Your shoulders stretched and then some more.
He wants his weeping, chastised whore to break apart,
in manicured hands, debutante,
he binds, commands. Your neck will quiver, bend,
acquiesce, venomous threats, felt and heard.
To make it quite clear, he will say it again —
pain you obey. "You will dance The Firebird."
You'll bleed in red feathers, pretend to be
free, but what's caged cannot stage liberty.

As You Become The Firebird

THE FIREBIRD

Clutching the hand of your mother, age 9
staring up at burning phoenix / elusive bird,
wooden wingspan stretched wide / ready to
engulf.

Imagine singe of hair become flame
scorching into ash / reborn again, magnificent
before your eyes, stretching bright / look away,
image branded across young eyes.

the flame has entered you / ball of white-hot light
singing from your chest / thumping heartbeat

memory is what you hold in mind as you practice,
become half bird/half woman, one phoenix –
the Firebird burning across stage / plummeting
through thin air / you are no limits,
weightless.

this is everything you worked to become / this
tingling flame / twinkle of light hung from sky.

Feet are talons arched and aimed to strike /
audience becomes prey / awed & open-mouthed
flaming light cast upon them / you are constellations
an entire solar system wrapped into bird-woman
this is all / you waited to become.

Sweat is Glitter

THE DOLL

on porcelain. This dressing room is doom
without a friend. Your Dior duffle found
aflame last week. Witnesses, crowded room,
nobody speaks. Brand new pointe shoes, nightgown
La Perla, lace trim, char, ash, all these gifts
from him — art director, collector of
long-legged things who crave attention with
expensive suffering. All gifts, but love,
including leading roles — even Firebird.
"It was never a goal." You tell the one
who dresses near you, ice blue eyes, few words,
suspicious — yet you have to trust someone.
She sweeps, swiftly, ashes into a bin.
She listens to you like she is a friend.

The Ladies are Waiting

THE DOLL

near guillotines, acclaimed headsmen of means.
Duplicitous gleams eyeing you, their thighs
secretly tattooed, surnames, killers, kings,
state-sanctioned blowjobs, beheadings so why
not princess — even you? One bed, one head,
misstep, or two, detected, collected, stored
fine wine uncorked, with lords, midnight, rust, red
aroma, royal deficiencies poured
in stone-floored cellars, behind arched oak doors.
A happy ending may require cunning,
a crown to topple, rolling heads on floors
ideally yours. Best sacrifice is queen.
Appeasement is the strategy you take.
They're carnivores, and you serve them cake.

v.

Diminish

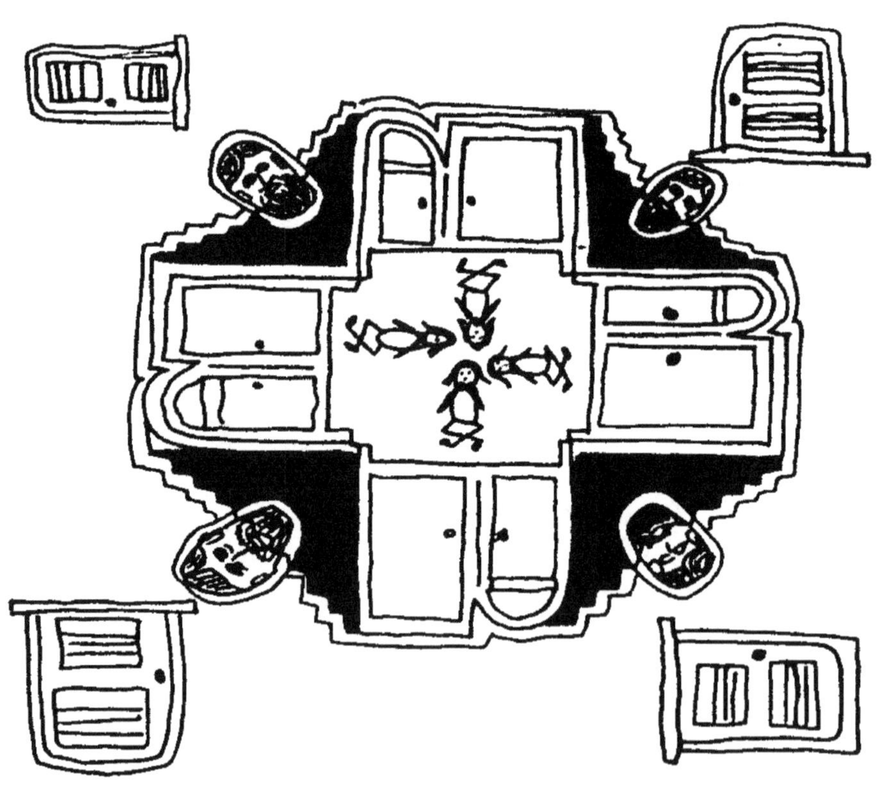

A Question of Size

THE WIZARD

All my life I've been running into people who declare, "Magic makes the world
a bigger place" as if conjuring greasy spells out of methamphetamine dust
and werewolf dandruff somehow gives your eyes binocular grace
dulls your narrowness
so you see the bigger picture, all the doors opening at once like a mansion
stricken with the flu
so you see the contents pour out like some silverware avalanche, debit card dysentery
all that sinful wealth melting like art when galleries catch fire
when brilliance gets slippery
it bores me to tears when other people want to make the world a bigger place
seems to me that they're simply settling for a bigger grave
death shouldn't get any bigger, understand me?
Sasquatch skyscrapers all around us, blurriness of glass windows
and drunk roofs in the hot sun
always blurry so you never know if it's truly broken or not
unless they slump to the ground
like the desperate animals they are, too many big things in this world of ours
overshadowing all the beauty still left to be found
big personalities wearing big robes stealing away sweetness
with empty words and little action, evil men who stab us in the cheeks
and sever us from magic
a world of dying dinosaurs who don't call themselves dinosaurs
who dress up like skyscrapers
who dress up like cities, who dress up like rulers with their fingers on
every trigger, every bomb
men who think they're gods, men who think they can grab meteors from the sky
shove the fire into their mouths, men who think that darkness is measured
in dollars and pounds
men who forget that smallness is the key to capturing the strength in trees
in bathroom sinks
a parade of purple spiders singing their songs up and down the streets
of a child's bedsheet
the specks of dust on unread books written by heroic witches
in the blood of their accusers
the stink of the wilderness, the brutality of green, a crucifix of crumbs
on the couch of our church
a crucifix that isn't really a crucifix, just two q-tips crisscrossed in martyr wax

candles that burn
smoke that burrows into earth, a catacomb of Marlboro Men
swapping cancers with cattle
holy farmland in the bedrooms of masturbators reading old catalogues
passed down from crones
loneliness is tiny, it's not what you expect, it's not an empire
walking on stilts wobbling in moonlight
in frightened kid flashlight, it's the dirt under fingernails, shadow on smartphone
loneliness isn't the ocean, not drowning, it's the puddle in your pantry
the crack in your vanity
the tiny things you keep in the attic of your brain, in boxes duct taped with veins
slammed tight
glued with a kiss, magic is a microscope not a telescope, it's the dollhouse
in the White House
death's diorama, the truth of magic, of mystery, smacked me in the marrow
one winter day
I found myself in a town on coastal America or maybe it was a village
of European bubble wrap
timeless have I gotten after all these years, it doesn't matter
I was drinking heavily from a ship in a bottle, all dizzy from bottled-up currents
tsunamis cracking through self-controlling corks
I found myself lost in a forest but it wasn't a forest, it was a hotel room
there were no trees
there were just the x-rays of trees scattered around the room like some crime lab
or monastery
the gray insides of so many trees, it was hypnotizing
these autopsies of sturdiness and bloom
I imagined me taking every tree ring I could find
and proposing to every man and woman outside
here is sappiness, I slip it on your finger, now you are to be married to the old world
celebrate
then suddenly I saw a light creeping towards me, it was coming from the bathroom
I swung open the door
expecting a beast but all I saw was a bathtub full of dolls and woodchips
no water
I stared in disbelief then in awe then the conjuring began in my dizzy head
routine went dead
there in a hotel room, in a forest of x-rayed trees, I finally experienced true magic true
tininess
helpless dolls drowning in a waterless sea of wood chips
the wilderness stripped to ligament
a world aiming to touch the sky will touch nothing at all

these dolls belonged to a better world
I wondered, how long did it take them to crawl to the tub
or who even brought them here
I decided then and there to build them a house
a lobotomy of wonder I would cut from air

Balletomane

THE DOLL

He binds you naked to a barren tree,
balletomane, smoke rings. Squinched eyes still sting.
Patient philosopher of cruelty
purchased boxed tulips to watch you practicing.

Pink areolas against silver bark,
a cloak, brunette, falls from your center part,
he lifts, licks pink outlines of shark teethmarks
bound ballerina drowning a mermaid heart,

aquarium he'll breathe to life. Stage door,
rapport a loud, intimate anonymity,
enters a womanchild in haute couture,
downcast dark eyes expect no family.

Sidewalk girl, smaller, off the stage, he sees.
He offers hands and walks to barren trees.

Upstaged

THE FIREBIRD

Nothing like the burn of lights swaying
across stick-thin body, muscles wrapped tight,
a flower waiting to bloom, petals held like fingers
gripping, reaching constantly to consume

you used to be the light of all his eyes, shimmering
but never enough — couldn't jump as high as desired
couldn't become the swan skating across lake-top glass;
she was the one who captured him. you snuck a glimpse
as he positioned her perfect body in pose, hands lingered
across the spaces you only dreamed for, yearning with
a deep burn, flames alight inside, this burning jealousy
like boiling lava steaming through veins, an itch you
cannot scratch, lack satisfaction — you're left on the
sidelines to watch as she, in flowing chemise, takes
whatever she pleases with an ease you will never possess.

Feet tiptoe across the floor, carry her like flight
as a ballerina you would never compare to her grace
natural and becoming, surrounded by light while you
worship the darkness blossoming inside
as the petals unfurl, you are a dark black rose
dripping ink; you will never be red as blood but only
burnt and charred inside, your heart ends flame
becomes ash scraped from floors swept by
those who come to clean vacant halls.

Elegy

THE DOLL

Such slick, new sheen on keratin, what's gone
is superficial, only skin, same heart
primeval, two horned tongue — the same
poison that you tasted young. Lethal art
her venom makes, near stranglehold of veins
that breaks with antidote of ancient wounds —
resistance to a childhood tomb. Disdain
she deigns an elegy, absolution
in shameful sympathy. This deity
with diamond head who whispers venom wants
you dead. Proximity without pity.
A hiss in neon grass of dreams that haunts.
Remakes herself a dozen summers new,
still slithers somewhere contemplating you.

The Girl at the Party

THE WIZARD

All parties are essentially the same, the really good ones are special in tiny ways
I've been to millions of parties, in secrecy on pilgrim ships or in the shadows
of New Amsterdam still-life, seemingly timeless cities surfing through the centuries
as horse bones give way to flat tires and the flickers of candles flock together
to form computerized fluorescence, cities where the fingers of its lonely peoples
still elongate
to touch smartphones stitched into space, loneliness hasn't changed at all
whether amoebas or Americas
millions of parties where the drinks are good or not, cheap
or made from diamond spit, caviar from kingly halls or roadkill from towns
where boys still can't kiss boys, parties where seasick clowns bang on drums
until the joke isn't funny anymore and they puke in kitchen sinks in apartments
where nobody knows nobody and if we're real lucky somebody will have a laptop
that's loud, that never dies and Spotify is truly a gift from the gods
of generational rifts and we'll all dance
until the cars parked outside are crushed beneath the weight of apocalyptic snow
or parking tickets, flimsy bureaucratic bibles that the wind simply blows aside
and we'll all laugh
these parties happen more often than not
but good parties have a few common denominators
a bunch of artists are losing their mind, it's the end of one world
and the weather outside cups your tongue and sits your eyes down in electric chairs
if you practice magic
it's easy to conquer any party
a little bit of charm and a few tricks and there's your crown
most of the time I'd appear to be levitating from man to woman
batting my eyelashes
zeroing in on their deepest wishes, extracting their insecurities
and turning them into ice cubes
chilling my drink with the Arctic of our humanity
and one time I was at this art party
and the warehouse looked like London but tasted like the tropics
but was probably inland
in America somewhere, everybody trying to impress everybody
and looking uncomfortable
the same way maggots do when they realize the body they're living in is not a corpse
but someone still breathing and not wanting angel wings

the awkwardness of biology not getting along with circumstance
and I was probably sprawled out on the makeshift couch
flicking spells at the walls and watching them bounce off
curious as to where they would go
what lips they'd crawl onto, laughing on the inside at how big
everybody was pretending to be
getting depressed at how humans ignore the tiny jewels inside them
that really make them shine
how everybody acts more like bloodless dolls rather than mammals
still hungover from too much evolutionary soup
how nice it would be if everybody were dolls in my dollhouse
at least then they could focus on what makes them different
special
rather than scraping by in the big world
then this dancer caught my eye
I knew she was a dancer because she was doing little pirouettes
over the ironic mirror glued to the blue-collar floor
she didn't think anybody was looking
she was merely practicing, preparing for her inevitable big dance
when the right song came on
so she could squash her jealous feelings and hypnotize everybody in the room
so they could melt into wax, into ash, into fog pouring out of shipwrecks
I finished my drink and grabbed somebody else's that was nearby
and swung my eyes back to the girl at the party
the dancer
who looked like a shipwreck that didn't know it yet
her hair long in certain lamplight but short in the moonlight
it seemed her hair changed depending on her mood
it'd be a long journey getting to know all her hairstyles all her moods
I wondered if she ever looked at airplanes as they fly over oceans
and wonder if they ever get jealous of shipwrecks
how they're cherished
haunting in a way that plane crashes could never be
people don't talk about planewrecks
before long, the right song came on
and the girl with shifting hair started to dance
all stopped

vi.

Wizards

When You First Meet The Wizard

THE FIREBIRD

She was a brilliant light that could
effortlessly defeat all-consuming darkness
you cocooned yourself in, did not know
anyone could exist who possessed
such a vision, had an innocence
you could not compete. and that was
your undoing – competition impossible,
no way for your light to shine beyond hers
and the way she danced with such grace
you could see the way he looked at her
the way he would never dream of you
tracing her body with feverish hunger
in ways you would only ever desire, afar.
murmurs came to me as you stood, fuming
after a flawless performance, he barely
noticed but someone else did, sent across
effervescent potion – chilled champagne.
you clutched the glass in one dainty hand
and swung your swan neck seeking the
anonymous admirer who appeared as if
out of water, forming into a solid apparition
before your eyes, gleaming. you'd never seen a man
such as him before, one look stole your breath;
"you're a stunning dancer" – just what you
needed to hear, as if he knew, as if he saw
straight through your soul. "not what some people
seem to think," a smirk over at the dancer
stealing all your light, twirling for a flock of
admirers. *"Some days, I just wish she would
disappear."*
Mysterious man cocked his head
in thought:
                    "I could make that happen."

She Whispers Wizards

THE DOLL

She whispers wizards. Blue irises dilate,
childhood compatriot who asks you on
a date, party, but she calculates —
a curiosity relied upon.

A wizard lured a girl from your high school,
post-graduation runaway. Kids could
be cruel with names for girls who flee with ghouls
to magic from suburban neighborhoods.

You never saw one but exchanged details
curated legends since pigtails — language
transforming mortals into beasts with tails.
Two grown schoolgirls sharing a pilgrimage.

She whispers wizards, old ardor she stokes,
this smiling girl who always smells of smoke.

Elixir

THE DOLL

A fuzzy thorax, freshly squeezed, an ooze
of fluid, fourteen bees. A massacre
mélange, minute, a concoction infused
with booze inside a champagne flute. A stir
a blur of bubbles, blood; tears, virgin, five
siphoned from last year's flood. A recipe
researched, for months, you found, college archives,
hometown to road trip hunt. Pale pet, pretty,
you must possess. A cut of crinoline,
a vintage wedding dress, you make a sieve
so she'll believe, a sip, love, first sight then
no risk, reprieve. Liquid through lace, must breathe,
then serve. A year of toil to make her swerve.
It boils a week this love you don't deserve.

NO.6
ELIXIR
Purified Extracts
booze-bubbles
blood-tears
virgin-s
blood
tears
blood
bubbles
tears
bubbles
blood

Potion to Shrink

THE FIREBIRD

In a dream, sneak away in cover of night
corsage tucked tight around pounding wrist
pulse thrumming through thick veins
powered by green poison, burning from the insides
this is the way it always was fated, from the start
the first moment you looked into her eyes
saw her growing, larger, becoming so much more
than you would ever be.
Travel to the ends of the caves and seek
darkness shrouding like a cloak
tiny bits of bejeweled starlight twinkle with each
sway of hips, your hair shifts, wraps around you
like feathers on skin. Greedy hands reach to
grasp at you and there you meet the Wizard,
dark and handsome, beard catches the light
of many moons and eyes like coal
among the shadows; perhaps it is his
hands on you, after all – he gives you
promises, understands you feel
overshadowed. Sympathizes.
Push on, stumble over words
tongue thick like leather and stifling
breath, you whisper in his ear
what you seek – *a potion to shrink.*
He knows exactly what you want to hear
as he whispers in your ear
the world glistens before your eyes
just think what it would be like
if you have no
competing sunrise.

Oscar Wilde Performs Surgery on the Wizard

THE WIZARD

This one time, Oscar Wilde removes my eyes with a silver spoon
and replaces them with Dorian Gray's eyes
he declares, "If eyes are windows to the soul... then let them be fictitious
may they never look old and tired"
we're in London of course
drinking wine made from grapes crushed into tears by homesick kangaroos
who escaped the outback looking for better job opportunities
"you can taste the harshness," Oscar explains to me
as he practices the fine art of swishing and spitting
but every time he spits into the spittoon, a little bit splashes into the grass
and I wonder how much human excess it would take for the grass to get liver disease
for its green to go yellow like mad kings in clock towers
for all of London to curl up into a ball that island kids kick around for a bit before they
get bored and decide to build a better world
I'm lost in thought when Oscar touches my arm
he wants me to throw my old eyes into the ocean
he wants them to sink to the bottom
he wants them to grow into trees that rise past the stalks of seaweed
he wants the suicides of navy boys to live out eternity plucking fruit from the branches
he wants the suicides of navy boys to grow up big and strong... like whales
then he wants them to rise to the surface and stare at the sun
and think about all the sex they missed out on
I tell Oscar he's drunk, but there's momentum in his madness
and he suddenly grabs my hand and declares, "We're going to a party
and everyone will love your new eyes"
I nod my head
"Yes"
Oscar's cute
I put my old eyes in the breast pocket of my suit coat close to my heart
because I've always been terrible at forgetting the things I've seen

All of us are made from old parts, we just tell ourselves that we're new
stories handed down from cloud to ground, some words take root and bloom
sometimes they're footsteps that don't make a sound, your eyes might get ripped from
your head
your nose might tell you that you're dead, there is music that smells
and stars that shrink at your touch, narratives that rough you up
and leave you broken, faces are forgeries that don't know what hope is

The Math of a Princess

THE DOLL

is there's just one of you — more in the corps,
a dozen girls, who covet the headpiece
secured by thirty bobby pins. Abhor
your good fortune. Pretend to be friends. Peace
is mathematically sound when it's ten
surrounding one too terrified, thin. Learn
survival means shopping, invitations —
one texting this evening, ice blue eyes burn
your soul: "Art party, castle, wear faux pink
mink stole. Tiara, I'll borrow — you've got
so many of them." No doubt she keeps track. Think
you should say no. Stay in. But it's a thought
that doesn't add up. You factor her wrath.
Too many girls hate you. It's princess math.

Castle Set Atop the Sand

THE FIREBIRD

You drive together, two ballerinas wrapped in
ribbons & lace, brightly colored bows looped through
strands of hair, silver threads that shine, tiaras
perched atop two heads, identical – finally friends.
You lifted the tiara from her bedpost, hanging like
a halo in fading light. she was always more of a
princess, more royal than you, but you know
that will all change tonight. the Wizard has called
upon you both for his weekly affair, a party in her
honor. Car puffs clouds, chugs along rocky path
tires grip & travel the incline, grass turns to sand
as you see the castle emerge from mist & clouds,
an apparition of desire, you are pulled toward it
as if enchanted already by the wizard's spell. You
gaze across at your companion, tight-lipped passenger
with look of dreadful mistrust, wide eyes grow bigger
at the sight of the castle set atop the sand,
magnificent with lust.

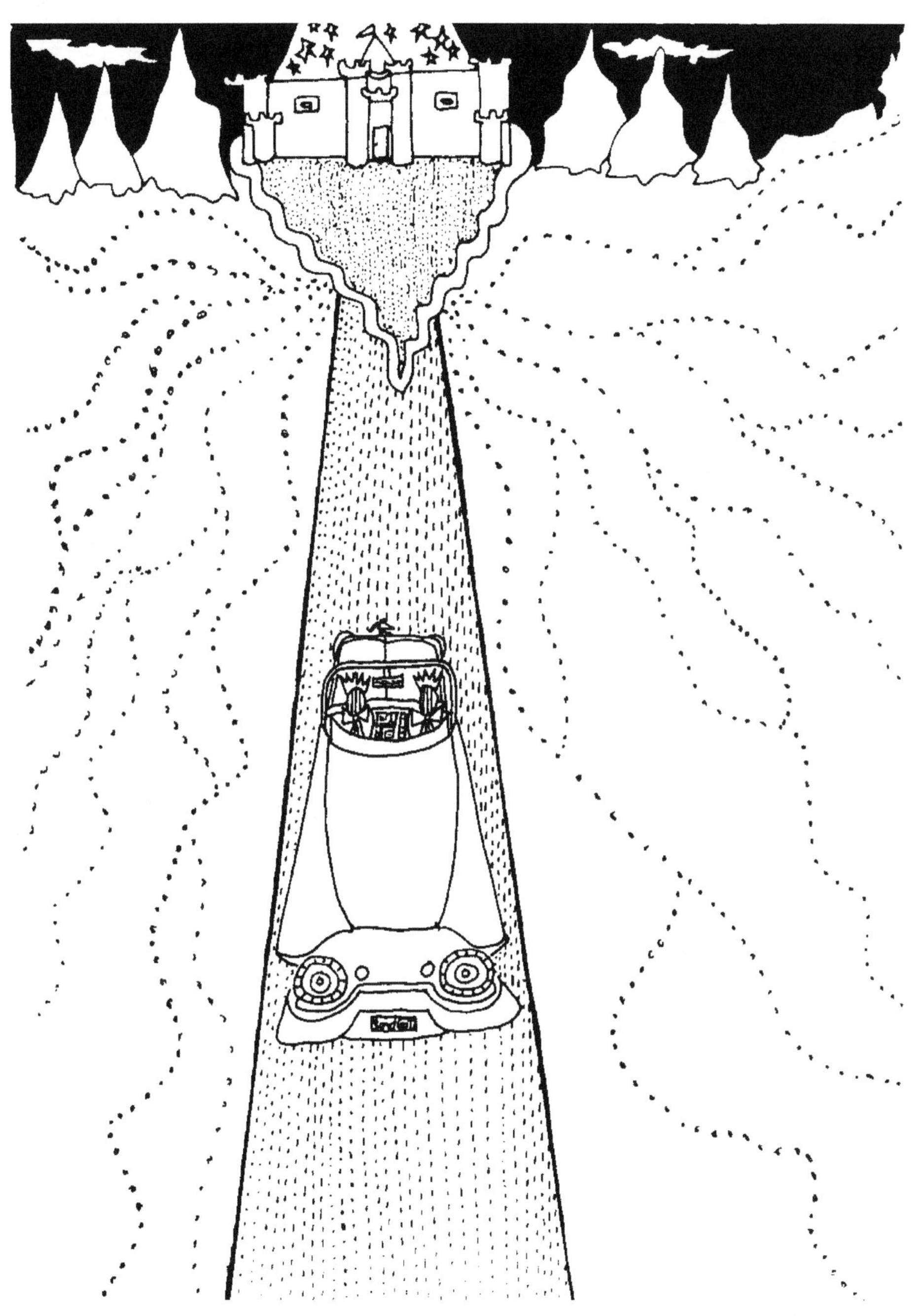

His Face When it Will Flicker

THE DOLL

is cracked glass Picasso striated grove —
skin branches, singed romances, flame buried
in bone chip snow, glycerine. Globe
revealing glistening cemetery.

His youth, a sunken mausoleum
mystery; angles become mangled. Face
is wasting, cubed. Happens in a wink.
You think you are confused — staircase

mistake of candlelight? Dim castle dire
as host, Adonis, promise, flickering
to ghost. Last crackle, dying fire,
a stranger you see magic, suffering.

His face when it will flicker licks your heart.
Cannot know the end. This is how it starts.

Skeletons

Her Skeleton was Shaped like the Stage

THE WIZARD

Once upon a time
a desperate werewolf asked me for the moon and I being a good friend said, "Sure"
so I sacrificed a bunch of virgin ladders, mixed their splintered blood
with pixie bones
and crafted a spell that would astronaut me to the satellite, so I was lifted there
like a ghost
when I had the moon in my grasp, the tidal waves twisting my toes
I had a change of heart
the whole moon would be too much, werewolf lobotomies
dead hummingbirds on windshields
revolutions trapped in basements, no blood in the attics of power
just mannequins masturbating
no, no, a sliver of magic must hang in the sky like a dead man
with a crystal ball for a head
so I sliced a chunk of moon and thought "good enough"
then the earth grabbed my feet
pulled me down into its continental drowning, gravity is a grave
where we bury our dreams
after crawling through ash, through a lingerie of fire ants
through mole men mortgages
all the werewolves were dead, extinct, the beasts in men
became something else entirely
so I was stuck with a piece of moon that I didn't know what to do with
so I turned it into a ring
so I wear it to remind me we should all be engaged to a future that's shimmering
an emptiness that can be filled
a destiny we can shrink down and hold in the palm of our hands
a messiness we can turn into music and the music can be our maps
so we're always looking for the thing that makes us tick
but I've always been a big schemer, which is why I own a castle on a hilltop
but it's not really hilltop, it's on a beach but there's no water, so it's not a beach
but there's sand
so it's a castle on a patch of desert and this patch of desert has delusions of grandeur
got it?
it thinks it's a beach and that's ok, but the castle is also part of a skyline of an old city
and this old city is proud of the new things it owns, got it?
it also looks like how the moon used to, back when there was more magic
in the world

I like throwing parties here
in my castle, which is also the moon, which is also a New York City apartment

Once upon a time
I met a ballerina, she came to this party I was throwing, it was a party for werewolves
but the werewolves are all dead, so I had all the guests kiss my moon ring
and I was hoping at least one partygoer would turn into one
and we can all howl again
nobody turned, which put me in a sorry state, but it was ok
because I couldn't stop thinking about that ballerina
I knew she was a ballerina, because her skeleton was shaped like the stage
her bones were meant to move, meant for grace, it was in her face
which had two eyes, of course it's a face, but her eyes were meant to conquer
and the rest of her face was just a casualty of that optical ambition
her eyes were dark, dark like coffee, the gas station coffee they throw away at the end
the coffee with character, the coffee that grips truckers
and chariot drivers by the calves
makes them buzz like dumb bugs lost in bright lights, her dark eyes were highways
swallowed up by the earth, I would go up and talk to her, give her a tour of my place
show her the dollhouse

Once upon a time I was bored
and traveled the globe in search of haunted dollhouses
I collected them all and smashed them to pieces
with the femur of a young woman who died during childbirth
I then took all the pieces and built a new dollhouse
Once upon a time
I showed the ballerina my dollhouse

Once upon a time I spit out a spell and there was a special drink
and the entire party drank
then there was the fall and most of the party went gone
but the ballerina was now small

Once upon a time I wasn't so crazy, I wasn't such an asshole

A Victorian Dollhousing Ceremony

THE DOLL

begins mixed drinks, faux friend who thinks you've grown
too big secretly meets some wizard with cash,
a stash, black lacquered porcelain
tea service, saucers dainty dimes, damask
cobalt wallpaper, flocked, cut dollhouse size;
its onyx flourishes matching dark eyes. Dyed
synthetic rhododendrons, vases he buys
online designer, custom, small. His pride,
pine hobby house, he built requires a doll
deposit tiny clawfoot tub. Reduced,
still breathing, by his drugs, to echoed calls
answered vast fingers through removed spruce roofs.
Cocktails, an art collector — "little things,"
You tasted drugs too late. You were shrinking.

Imagine: Dancing Solo

THE FIREBIRD

Tempting invite becomes more than first desired,
one sip of the elixir and it begins —
watching her shrink beneath his dark spell
you sip your drink and smile, imagine
the sparkling lights as you dance onstage
solo soaking in the beams, applause, feeling
his eyes on you, only you now.
she can no longer steal your spotlight,
she may dance as she pleases but no more
will she rise as you fall; the wizard your ally
in this dark endeavor, you may now dance
freely, uninhibited to claim your fantasy.
a full-grown woman, voluptuous curves and
long legs crisscrossed, wrapped in jet-black fishnets
hair perfectly wrapped in brilliant tied bow
bouncing atop her head as she diminishes, becomes
tiny — you never imagined she would actually
be as the wizard said, miniaturized and minute
so tiny you can barely see her disappearing
before your eyes, disguise as reality grips
tightly, claiming her to live in dollhouse forevermore
prepared, set tabletop center in Victorian glory
fresh pine shavings from creation, onyx trappings
details designed to give illusion of entire world
miniaturized just like her — magic potion to shrink
worked in a single wink, dwindling like wilted rose
furling into herself caving in, still breathing and
fated to live lonesome, solitary and companionless
blank-eyed dolls clustered round walls watch her
expressionless, emotionless and lip locked,
unmoved as their new resident is born.

The Unfamiliar Music of Mermaids in Snow Globes

THE WIZARD

This one time I was wandering in a different hemisphere
came across a seaside pawnshop on a Japanese isle
the man there was selling these hypnotic snow globes
inside each snow globe was a tiny mermaid crying out for freedom
when you shook it, the mermaid's eyes would flare up with hope
it was quite beautiful, thinking your optimism is what cracks glass
thinking your dreams of the future breaks the bars of your cage
the demented pawnbroker told me the mermaids were only taking naps
naps with their eyes open, naps that would protect them
until the world was a better place
naps that lead to maps, maps that you wear on your feet
to get you to where you need to go
because the world right now doesn't understand beauty
doesn't understand the delicacies of curves you can't feel
we must turn the living into ghosts and tear down the houses that haunt them
then we must take that rubble, grind it into dust
use the dust to make skins that the ghosts will wear and be alive again
I was blown away, the idea of shrinking beautiful things to hide them
from an ever-growing ugly
an ugly world always looking for them, always looking to straitjacket their lip-breaths
always looking to shove their sunset slides into a sanitarium of stillness
I turned the pawnbroker into a starfish, shoved him into a cannon
and shot him at the sky
now he's a part of a constellation that whips fishermen and young lovers into frenzy
I really hope he thanks me, I really hope he appreciates the glow I stuck him to
after I disposed of him, I took all the mermaids in snow globes
and one day I'll let them loose
into bathtubs of flower spit
or maybe an antidepressant lake of rock where all the tears have hardened
maybe that's why I shrunk down the dancer, used magic to confuse
that girl with disloyal hair
I never thought it would work, these shrinking spells, but they did
and now here we are
the naked dancer who shrank through her clothes
sleeping in the master bedroom on the top floor of my dollhouse
the girl with the changing hair staring at a wall in the basement
I have to ask myself, "Am I a monster?
Am I a sociopath? Should the world get rid of me?

Why hasn't it yet?"
I don't have time for such questions or maybe it's all a lie and I'm scared of the truth
anyway, I should get a tiny brush for the one
something classy for the other
maybe the choker with the velvet collar
with a cameo
the one of Medusa with the snakes
the snakes that look like wings
I'll put her in it, maybe she'll like that
it's funny how big your fingers are when your world gets smaller
they run like monsters across hardwood floors
they shake like an earthquake, a song you think you've heard before
but you can't remember the title and you worry you'll take that mystery to the grave

Childish Skeleton

THE DOLL

It is night soon & then it is fall.
The gods against me in this
garish season are waning
with the heat. A skeleton
asleep, my soul found refuge
in a pornography of thorns,
the manicured mania
of wilting & weeds,
words made me believe
to be a meadow.
Kind I found, afloat,
red-eyed, choked, chased
by him, closed eyed,
sweating, heaving, drooling bride
at five—kept me alive
an anonymous adolescence,
a brooding bitching bloom
bewitched in its verdant womb,
convalescence/evanescence,
erasing massacre, inner thighs,
blooming dandelions in brown eyes.
Young becoming wild enough
to flee & be, maybe, free
& you would deceive me.
The shame is of the season.
The art is in the ache.
You found a childish skeleton.
I wasn't hard to break.

I have been broken many times

THE FIREBIRD

I am not fragile, but I have been
broken many times before. I have
shattered in a million pieces
un-fix-able,
yet still risen from
the debris, rubble pile of
disgrace and shame, silenced
to keep the truth from bubbling
out of my lips like acid, spat in faces
of my attackers, those who have instilled
this shame, who never saw the
truth, neglected my body, my soul,
my self; made me feel I am
nothing.
no-thing.

viii.

Paper

Parchment Doll

THE DOLL

Brimstone basement, his paper doll, as pale
as parchment, cut to crawl. A pencil brown
begets a veil of hair. Cornflower, frail,
survivor's stare.   Beneath, in dark she drowns
each night, a mattress bare, deadbolt locked tight
below symphonic terrors he creates:
the hounds that haunt her, screams then pleas contrite.
All naked nightmares, a drought of dreams, her fate
a flurry of erotic extremes. Squeak
on stairs, summons from sleep. Upstairs what waits
is horror on repeat — he twists and tweaks.
Diorama designed to keep her in,
his doll for parchment torture without end.

Paper Thin

THE DOLL

Inside red-curtained bed, you try to lift
a parchment head. Neck crinkles as it yearns
with vellum, veinless arms, then burns; so swift
you hear the tear — a ripping as you learn
you've flattened everywhere, while you were asleep.
Too fibrous now to weep, you could
disintegrate, wet, weakened. Frown, demure,
even a risk that you would wrinkle should
he kiss, the wizard who did this, shrunk, turned
you paper thin, between his fingers bend
a crumpled doll, dissected, either spurned
returned limbs taped to take apart again.
Paper dolls cannot hear their lungless screams,
and that is how you know it was a dream.

What the Sky Looks like Right Now

THE WIZARD

Sometimes I pretend the sky & clouds
are just pieces of really expensive paper

shooting stars are just really beautiful papercuts

when you're young
you stare at the sky & write with your eyes
imagination is just a really nice optometrist
who encourages your vision even if it misses the mark

as you get older
you stare at the sky & write with your fists
it's a little more violent

you dream of rocket ships exploding in earth's atmosphere
jet lag confetti raining down on rooftop parties
where evil men drink hallucinogenic bourbon
out of the skulls of orphan babies

you dream of planes crashing into gated communities
where the rich never leave their mansions
spending most of their time
ripping out pages from chapbooks
written by overworked poets
always on the verge of suicide
making paper airplanes out of the trauma
throwing them into fireplaces

when you're old
you don't even look at the sky
every room in your home
in your heart
in your brain
has become a basement
full of wet boxes
caused by leaky pipes
you don't bother to repair

all the suicide notes & love letters
you've penned over the years
disintegrating into mush
the words that meant so much
running into one another
like when cops break up a party

the words left behind
form new sentences
you must dig out of the drowning
then you must read what you sew:

there are no windows in your life anymore
all the lovebirds stuffed into a drawer

tenderness is a thousand dolls taking your breath away
a thousand cats pulling your ribcage like a sleigh

the death you deserve, fireflies sinking to the bottom of an ashtray
you've always been an origami car stranded on the highway

and the sun is always setting somewhere else
you just wanted a hotter melt

Paper Houses

THE FIREBIRD

Stacked up high, shreds of torn paper
crinkled after hours spent making
papier-mâché mansions,
entire dwellings for your dolls.
Every girl may have this memory
but you - you would burn the houses
after painstaking time crafting each
unique details; you couldn't allow
a single creation to exist intact,
burnt them all down and watched
the flames demolish the dollhouses
inside. Sometimes dolls don't make it
out unsinged. You watch their yarn hair
ignite, feel the heat of the fire consuming
plush bodies, acrid smoke of burning hair
and melted wax skins. Your mother would
scold you for starting fires again
you hid the matches in a secret pocket
planning your next burning. When you could
next see the flames, imagine how it'd feel
if that heat burrowed deep in your bones.
Beneath your skin. All the power that existed
in a single flickering flame, all that
you could consume
with that power.

Paper Kitten

THE DOLL

A paper ball is breathing in your bed.
Translucent ribcage, a folded head. Ears
rotating at the sounds, a dreamy head
discerning what it's found. It wasn't here

when your eyes shut. It stretches a washi spine,
reveals red dot birthmark, a paper cut —
you understand this gift, pet, was designed
by his own hands, in mustard/butternut,

just one enchantment at the end, purview
of magic men, incantation to make
it breathe, to twitch a tail enough that you
believe in magic, forgive his mistake.

A paper kitten he enchants to breathe,
a little life he leaves for one you grieve.

ix.

Dollhousing

Cameo

THE DOLL

His body coiling, snakeskin bow, your neck
black velvet, he's surrounding slow. First gift,
affixed accoutrement, oval reflects
a fate you scry by accident. Silk shift,
a shuffle, half asleep, you feel its tight
reminder creep across pulsed vein constrained
with lock. You claw its fabric, frozen, fright,
a shock at midnight, mirror, scalloped frame,
a serpent, panic, suffocating pain.
Abalone visage, curling hair floats
on amber, side-eye stare. A warning skeined
around your throat, a shell of girl who chokes
connotes brutality or jewelry?
You're locked inside either respectively.

Visiting Dolls

THE FIREBIRD

Sneaking into a Wizard's home offers risk
to a high degree, Dalmation guarding doors;
toss a juicy steak to occupy his jaws and slide
inside, feet pattering soft like any ballerina does
like a dance with no audience, swinging your body
into a dead-silent house, you want to reach her, his
living doll. not sure what your plan is once you do,
kidnap this macabre creation or kill it before it can
destroy you, your allure once seemed enough but you've
come to realize, he never wanted you, it was always her.

he keeps her in the sunroom which reflects moonlight
piercing beams straight to your heart. creep across to
darkened dollhouse; one ring of light shimmers
in the center like a beating heart, or sliver of moon.
upstairs in a Victorian draped bedroom lies the shrunken
ballerina, perfect as ever even 10x less her size.

creak of floorboards alerts too late, you've barely caught a
glimpse before you feel him, sinister shadow crawling overtop –
you are in his sights, bullseye, your heart tremors knowing
he could kill you in an instant or shrink you down to
mousetrap size - you've heard tales of a wizard who could
capture mermaids in a globe of glass, who could
turn men into starfish without a thought.

Dark Magic curls its finger at you, beckons alluring and seductive –
you hear him calling to you, he is below... turn from the dollhouse,
tiny dancer dreaming anything but peaceful, tossing and turning
in a miniature world.

follow his dark pull through halls, black and blind. reach
for something to grasp, nothing — entering a black hole.
feet hit stairs, he calls you to join him, below,
beneath the earth, a secret cavern belching from
the house's belly and why are you surprised a wizard's
home has a mind of its own? your body automatic heads

down
down
down, smell of earth and...
dead dreams reside here.

glimmer off glass in one corner of the room,
walls close around you – congested, cobwebs
wrap you like film around thin arms, claiming
your ability to dance for their own.

this darkness is a human, breathing, beating heart
and you are now a basement dweller, door
closes above behind you, fear you will
never see the light again.

you will never
see the light.

The Second Time You See Marie Taglioni
(the peg doll ballerina of Princess Victoria)

THE DOLL

it sits. You spy through slits the button back
mahogany armchair. Enchanted flames
backlight a black dot stare, lace headdress. Wrack
your addled head, lumbering limbs, for names —
decrypting decades, dolls recalled. Peg feet
hand-painted pink by princess without friends —
you, 10, first European trip replete
with castles, dolls. You held this one pretend,
cheap paper imitation, elation —
frustration, ripped before returning to
predictable use, prosaic nation.
Royal abduction before he took you,
who struggles, drugged, retaining thought in thrall
and holds his first — even most precious doll.

The Eye

THE DOLL

Dollhouse will dim when he commands goodnight.
Six chandeliers, nine candelabrum cede
enchanted light. All die but pillar, slight,
beside your bed, brick candle wax free bleeds
eight hours in a magician's stead. He leaves
his proxy flame, perpetual night light,
a circle cipher in a canopy
that maps good girl geography. Respite
red curtains, bridal lace bedspread, a wet
embroidered pillow for a weepy head.
Eyes half open/awake with fear, regret,
a bedroom window peek pulls wide with dread.
Unblinking terror magic magnifies,
a familiar squint, ice-blue, female eye.

X.

Fingers

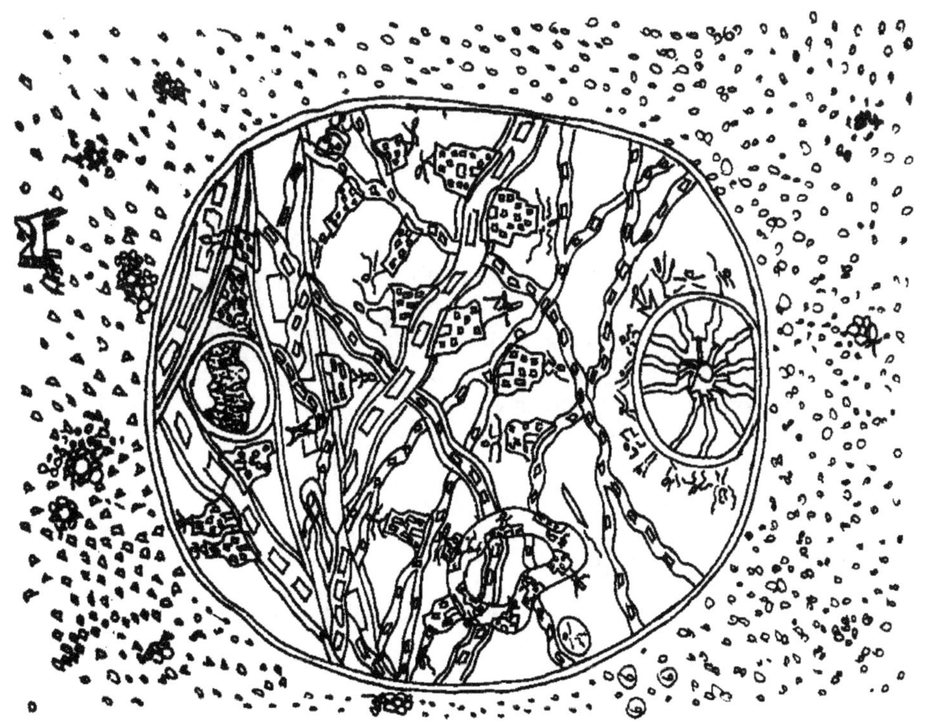

A Confession of Madness and a Glass of Bordeaux

THE WIZARD

Fingers are monsters, hands are storms, they clench
and shipwrecks bubble from knuckles and children are turned into orphans
and little birdies are tortured, wings go wrong and sun goes moon
and dark slams into light and someone somewhere gives up the fight
too many pills, too many potions, too many thrills, but too much peace
and dance floors don't dream, chaos uncrutches broken legs
and plucks dawn from peach pits, rise my sun from turntable glitz

too many spells, because our fingers are monsters
my own fingers running through the dollhouse
causing quakes that wake the tiny dancers
and I don't know why I'm doing what I'm doing
but something good must come from this madness
it has to or I've lost my heart
whatever Wi-Fi connection I have to human kindness

look, there's this New England tribe of hipsters
that eat seaweed and vomit in truck-stop bathrooms
the seaweed clumps together in plumbing pipes and become flesh
Olympic swimmers soaring through fast food guts and catwalk confetti
what we can do with the bones we've been given
and it has to be good
or we're doomed
I need to figure out what the fuck I'm going to do

a dancer in the bedroom, a dancer in the basement
one naked like the air and the other pulling at her hair
I must clothe the one, calm down the other
buy me some time with a haunted cameo
pour myself a glass of Bordeaux
drink, think
we must all learn how to glow
and maybe a good wind will blow
maybe all this will be worth it
maybe I'm not an asshole
maybe I won't die enflamed in spit

Tiny Type

THE DOLL

Inside a dollhouse you lose track of time,
explore interiors to occupy
the mind. A week, third floor, you're self-confined,
before downstairs you tip-toe terrified.

You open a library, second room,
auspicious, ovalular discovery,
a rolling ladder ride round aged volumes —
pages, torture, absent typography.

You drown your sorrows, low, hand-hooked rug sea,
alive girl consigned to apathy, tears
a spying wizard through window will see.
Pages flutter. He mutters. Words appear.

Elation, turning pages, black on white,
he's turned your emptiness to tiny type.

Silence

THE DOLL

is seamless, Victorian nightgown, roof
reproof, no fingers or electric sounds
when it's affixed, lightless chandeliers, proof
of fealty, microscopic tears.   Hound
haunts fears, your plate glass tabletop front lawn,
barks at shadows, windows, doors while the hand
is gone. Perimeter once stood upon
with plastic hedge, inch edge to tile crash land
or Dalmatian whose lunging signal, teeth
remands to silent walls without a back --
turntable, aerial attack. Relief
the latter, only friend, through shingles black
the five descend desiring fingerplay.
His fingertips are all you'll hear today.

Basement Dreamscape

THE FIREBIRD

All around you nests worldly treasures, archives of
mysticism and impossibility, more a freakshow of
         trapped desires and dreams
floating into existence with sheer wizardly will
you are nothing more now than a bottled wonder
exhibit to be shown, gazed upon. No longer
real to the outside world. you once dreamed of
         burning
and becoming magnificent with your flames
perhaps you are a witch yearning for the stake
to feel the burn across slick skin instead of
         consuming all inside.
Crackling and sparking, popping heat & bones
hair furling flames, hissing Medusa snakes
eyes are stone, blue ice condemns foes
you splinter into shards of red-hot glass
     a creature caged
cannot be kept. You will be Free. You will.

The Body is a Poem You Will Die Inside

THE DOLL

The leg is a riddle,
decrepitude chides.
Its lift, lamentation,
the last of your pride.
The pain is a lover
inside you who died.
The dance is dementia
devouring its bride.
Your dress swan feathers
dripping formaldehyde.
This stage is a suffering
you must abide.
Your moon has a womb,
an orbit blue-eyed.
The dark, its monarch,
is complicit beside.
Window lattices movement,
quarters your pride.
Your meager desperation
a larger universe spies.
The beast bares tall teeth
pink jowls, jaws wide.
His master a question
masquerading as guide.
In bed, curtained red,
you scream to a mutual sky.
Two lips, miniature, quiver
configure one word — why?
This house holds his secrets
it, one night, confides —
the body is a poem
you will die inside.

Orphan Dust, Stardust and Angel Dust

THE WIZARD

I never planned for any of this and I know that sounds like a cheap way out
but it's the truth and now there's this tiny dancer hiding in a dollhouse armoire
now there's a woman in the basement dancing with herself as if in a trance
I gave her a single rose and I don't know why, maybe an exit strategy
or one last dance
but she didn't budge, maybe a mirror on the wall I couldn't see
or maybe I'm losing it
the one in the dollhouse is frightened to death, I'm not sure why
I even made her small
I didn't think it would even work, magic is strong, but it's getting weaker by the day
I'm probably dying, I don't know even know old I am, one last gasp before the ocean
becomes an obituary, before tenderness gives way to sandpaper
before bone betrays flesh
and marrow betrays bone and the yesterdays in our brains suffocates the tomorrows
in our hearts, when there's no future anymore, just pyramids, strip malls and cafes
just orphan dust, stardust and angel dust, a splattering of regret
on the painter's canvas
no more enchantment, just a long walk through the dark until we're done, what to do
but shrink a bouquet into something she can grasp, maybe then she'll see
I'm not all that bad
present her with that haunted cameo, put it around her neck
maybe a nightgown for her to wear
this isn't the wilderness, no Genesis aftertaste, no purity in exposure, this is a world
where cruel men still pull the strings, obsessed with vulnerable things
nothing left to share
I thought I was different, now I'm not so sure, she's frightened in the armoire
she probably thinks I'm a monster, why did I concoct a drink
that makes beauty small?
why didn't I die centuries ago? An orphan like me should never have lasted this long
I got ambitious with magic and now feel bad about it, I should be burning in hell
gone
like the empires of old, her tears will be the end of me, as it should
can I turn this all good?
and the one in the basement is staring at the wall, not really a basement
more like a dungeon
where I store all my hungers that have imprisoned me, not really a dungeon

more like a museum
where I store all my possessions, artifacts from golden ages, fairytale taxidermy
oh nonexistence
aquariums and kiddie pools full of water from rivers that don't exist anymore
mermaids having parties in the bellies of dead whales
blood-covered turntables plucked from pirate ships
whatever down there should eventually see the light of day
newborn babies in a million cribs
I can't horde all the beauty that's left in this dying world, but who else will protect it?
no government in any hemisphere, certainly no politicians straddling equators
priests who perish
bros who bludgeon
and what of the orphans of today?
tattooed onto flash drives, digitally lost
abandoned by history and floating like ghosts through the pages of spell books
new ghosts
fossilized ghosts
poets below the earth
supermodels on high
and here we all are and it's hard
trying to keep the light alive
having to do the tough thing to make the goodness last
I ache

A Single Rose is Survival

THE FIREBIRD

thorn-clad stem extends from outstretched hand
peace offering, a symbol of old-time romance
you don't reach out to accept, continue staring
at lucid dreamscape painted across one wall
no way to tell if it's a product of magic or real
this mermaid staring back at you, holding your gaze
you have fallen into her embrace of gentle eyes;
evokes sympathy for the living doll above, listlessly
dancing away in her doll-sized mansion, perfect
as she always was, the role of dreams assigned
to your sole rival; still she takes the center stage,
still she steals your light and you are here, below
making silent friendships with enchanted mermaids
trapped behind thick glass, bubbles rise from kelp
lips, serene siren smile, you are captivated in this
unspoken melody reaching softly to your ears
alone—

kill your competition, it sings, and that is the
moment you know:

one of you, the doll or the firebird,
must be destroyed for the other
    to survive.

All the World's a Stage, Except When It's Not

THE WIZARD

She is a dancer, not *was*
you can't clear a history of passions like you can with pornography on the computer
it is who you are
like a permanent turtleneck of leeches wrapped around your heart
always draining you dry

the tiny dancer frightened in the armoire needs to dance
it's what she was born to do
maybe a stage will unfrighten her scares, stabilize the situation
so I rummage through a billion attics grabbing all the tarot cards to use for the stage

like a house of cards, but better, a stage built on the otherworldly ash of evil men
tarot cards made from the ash of Christian crusaders as they stared
at crosses of personal Jesus
tarot cards made from the ash of Puritan bros as they dreamt up
new ways to torture witches
tarot cards made from the ash of Jack the Rippers as they chased after angel hookers

I followed their ectoplasmic Frisbees into hell where they sneezed ash for all eternity
I collected their ash in Ziploc baggies, on earth I plucked fortunes
from the fallen testosterone
started building a giant stage somewhere in the deserts of America
because all the world's a stage, except when it's not

and I imagined great cities all over the world, cities built more like stages
imagine a Broadway musical where women and children stomp out their songs
on tarot cards
so their anger, their sadness, would reverberate in the afterlife
and evil spirits would suffer
I was a better man back then, idealistic and vengeful, but the plan never materialized

war broke out or maybe there was another depression
maybe we just didn't call it *great*
and I shoved all the ashy tarot cards into attics and thought I'd never see them again
but here we are and there's this tiny dancer who needs a stage
who may want revenge

so I whip up a couple of spells and magically glue all the tarot cards together
they float

and fist together, because the anger is real, then they do something unexpected:
the stage goes circular and a winding wheel appears playing music
there are three flats too
and what appears to be ornate wallpaper adorned with dark flowers
then I shrink it down
until it can fit into the dollhouse and the music playing is also unexpected:
Depeche Mode

but not Depeche Mode, a cover of their song "Behind the Wheel"
by Maxence Cyrin
tickling ivories and it's New Wave done elegant, like a waltz
a waltz done in a spaceship
and I always thought that one day I'd be piloting a giant piano through space
an explorer squashing the silence of the universe
that comets would waltz with other comets

just because my fingers flicked, just because the music of humanity
can do special things
just because our dancing is worth saving, that we must never forget
the rhythm of anguish
how we twist our bones to convert anguish into art, how that art can transport us
to a better place
where streets are paved with tarot cards and there are no tears
and every rooftop is a dancefloor.

Wet

THE DOLL

He rubs his thumb against two other ones,
index and next, fingertip circles slow
until it flows — honeysuckle scent from
some dripping aperture, brass faucet. Knows
by rote the bubble height you like — that steam
makes nightmares dreams, cleans freshly shrunken dolls.
How intimate submerging naked seems,
even in microscopic extremes. Small
enough to float atop his palm, you're calm
but wet. Forgetting he's the reason you
are here, so nearly disappeared, embalmed,
enchanted water fingertips drew
from sorcery, dew — yet something small survives.
Fingers make you remember you're alive.

A Ghost Escapes

THE DOLL

which hides inside eyelids, an armoire — grown,
alone, his captive hidden, destiny
unknown, eerily familiar — cloned bones,
solipsistic moans, the iniquities
of phantasms, ascension through ribcage
first time behind pine louvered closet doors,
a whore for chasing, erasing since age
five. Babydoll deprived forevermore
autonomy, memory but alive —
surviving, sometimes even thriving yet
the driving force within her is to find
the smallest spaces where she can forget.
A ghost escapes, well-trained, the brain's trapdoor,
skeleton you abandon here once more.

The Eyes Have You

THE DOLL

Some folded skin holds you in, eight-hour twitch
within, recumbent, witch who rides you to bliss,
her broom across pocked moons through violence --
oblivion. Her orbicularis
oculi tight as thighs, escape denied --
just iris tremors, whimpers. Dithering
in blackholes dilated, you hide inside
arachnid-legged pale lids, a withering
phantasm made midnight slave. Behave
until the dawn when what's sublimated
is gone. She becomes something you couldn't save,
a cotton candy sacrifice, a bed
to remember moments before the grave.
Each day, farther away, she says goodbye.
She rides you every time she shuts her eyes.

Please, Please, Please Bring Us a Dream

THE WIZARD

Long ago there was an alleyway in every American city
where teenage girls made of sand sold baggies of other people's dreams
dreams that look like radioactive Ritz Crackers, but taste like metal dental tools
it was not a fulfilling experience, but in the end we're all fools
dissatisfied with the music in our own heads and we're desperate to bring in
a better band
so we all do whatever it takes to get electricity back in our bedbug brains
a shock to your temple
on your knees mouthing prayers
like you're vomiting planes until the smoggy sky trembles

these day, there aren't too many teenage girls made of sand
that kind of magic is done
these days, there are toxic boys spraying them with water guns
all dreams are almost gone
I remember when the sky was flowery and not smoggy
when there weren't any desperate planes
just vengeful witches on broomsticks
flinging rabid cats with sharp claws into royal bedrooms
attacking kings, starting revolutions
shredding tyranny to pieces, skulls of men in cauldrons

these days, there are trails of kitty litter where beaches once were
these days, witches are in hiding and the sky is a giant teardrop looking for a cure
now that you can't buy dreams on the street, you must conjure them
between the sheets
and invade the unguarded brains of those deep in sleep
and one night I'm bored
and not knowing what I should do with the tiny dancer
I decide to see what she sees when the curtain falls

imagine a New York club in the 1970s
an army of disco punks ripping out their hearts and hitting cops with them
imagine the glitz and grime of Bethlehem, the purity of mayhem
martyrs with snakes for arms dancing around a crown of thorns
still life lepers learning how to shake off their germs
imagine the weird sisters from Macbeth doing meth and curb stomping creepy priests
and then all churches undress and become beasts

and then the music stops
and then there are chalk outlines in puddles of holy water
and they're trying to dance, but they can't
all seems lost, but it isn't
imagine that the beasts are killed by daughters in shining armor
and patriarchy crumbles into dust
imagine witches climbing off their stakes and through the flames
and they smoke big cigarettes and blow deathly cock rings onto Puritan men
and they lose their sex and America ends before it even began
and the world is reconfigured
and the witches
who aren't really witches
start an empire of imagination that cleans up the ocean's sadness
wiping away the tears with tissues as big as the sky
until the ocean isn't deranged by its depression anymore
and so you can't drown in it anymore
and it's more like a desert
and then this bewitching empire forces the desert to realize how much
of an asshole it is
until it cries so much it's no longer a desert

now I'm lost in her dream
now she's in control
now I'm twisting in her music box
now she's taking out a knife that looks like a spaceship
now she's carving into my stomach
now she's pulling out a statue of who I used to be
now she's crushing it into a fine dust
now she's sprinkling it into my eyes
now I'm going blind

He Knows What You Did in a Dream

THE DOLL

Sometimes your dream requires CSI — gleaned
evidence, machete eye, his silver grey,
remembered green. Steel glinting iris clean-
wiped-blade must mean he knows, yesterday,
you murdered him — inside your head, white gown,
blue velvet trim, asleep, serated knife
shaped like a mothership, you found
in shaking fingertips, to take his life —
or so it seemed. You wake, no blood, outlines
in chalk or screams just silver eyes outside
a bay window. Huge fingers tremble, sign
he somehow knows. That innocence has died
is chemiluminescent on dollhouse walls.
The truth in darkness glows like luminol.

Seducing a Dying Wizard

THE WIZARD

It's like being drunk, my fingers running through the dollhouse
knocking over everything
I don't know what's happening to me, the clumsiness, the heaviness of city
infrastructure weakening over time, potholes replacing my eyes, my mouth a bridge
collapsing in the middle
my nose a public school rotting from the inside out, ears like playgrounds
turned into drug zones

in the right light, see the obituaries tattooed all over my body
different versions of myself
I've killed over the years, but nothing like this, body abandoning brain
brain bored with body
or my brain like a hot air balloon with a poked hole, magic leaking out
wind flaps bones
no control, fingers like tectonic plates giving the dollhouse the shakes, all the tiny
mirrors break but the tiny dancer is calm like a beach without any waves
with no monsters to make any graves

she's in control, my fingers are poles, my fingers are toys, I'm now the animal, death to
all boys death to the old world, now my fingers are at a loss for words
the tiny dancer moves real slow
she takes my skeleton and pushes through, clothes like van Gogh
dress new Prussian blue
black cameo squawking like a crow, velvet bodice falling to the floor
hormones in a zoo breaking down the bars, she's naked now, my fingers are hers
so I imagine the stars
what they looked like when I was young, never imagined I would end up like this

Fingers

THE DOLL

Undressing you without caressing you,
they're fumbling while unbuttoning a black
cameo appliquéd new Prussian blue
dress. Chest against fierce fingertips, impact
knocks back its panting doll to tiny French
armoire, hard nipples reduced goosebumps, shards.
A velvet bodice, fallen guard, you wince,
all wet remembrance, tunnel pleasures, schoolyards,
backseats of vintage cars, even at barres,
a hollowed inner thigh correction, spied
by jealous eyes. Romanticized each touch
& terror 'til today, arched back, legs wide
an offering too minuscule to clutch.
These fingers linger, lurking, far away
at the fireplace until you will obey.

THE DOLL

xi.

Enlightenment

What Becomes of a Garden

THE DOLL

You notice it's empty first time you hide,
black oak French armoire, naked inside, like
you in its corner, breathless, petrified.
Blossoming tutu, blue buds crowning thighs,
from flourish, fingers, bouquet he blooms, skirt
of tulips hydrangeas dripping doom, rose
prestidigitations of petals flirt
against yours — dewy, pink. Perfume follows
fear, twirling, trying hard not to think — what
becomes of gardens when frost withers blooms?
How many dances, years, wilting, walnut
ballrooms before, in dollhouse, you're entombed?
You open for him, fresh, fragrant with fright.
What becomes of a garden tonight?

His Music Box Breathes Depeche Mode

THE DOLL

a hollowed set design inside dollhouse
ballroom. Five fingers lead. Wallpapered flats,
black bloomed, encircle stage. Gossamer flounce,
gray ballet skirt, a plié romance danced,
piano wound by fingertips, Behind the Wheel
tuned teeth play Maxence Cyrin. Planet eyes,
constellations, melt, stratosphere surreal
inconstant asteroid belt, light devised
stings limbs like lust. A moonbeam pas de deux,
move as you must, his passenger. Fouettés,
regrets, releasing whim, each orbit you
spin closer to him for God the father
created little girl and universe;
his music box breathes, and you will rehearse.

A Lonely Wizard's Enchanted Lighter

THE FIREBIRD

Moments of weakness where you can feel
his presence no longer as strong, when the wizard
does not hold you away from harm; his grip
slackens and you can be free, exploration is yours.
escape the Wizard's captive spell to lurk
unnoticed through his home, peering between
cracked doorways, climbing winding staircases
in this castle of mazes. one room, pristine, the
heart of it all, his nesting grounds - bedroom
with arching four-post and feathered pillows
tempts you to burrow in and rest among
the privacy of a wizardly soul, his hearth glows,
fireplace lit with mystic flames, heat reaches
like prying fingers, stringing you further inside.
there – on the bedside, glistening oyster pearl
keepsake, polished silver plate glinting —
how one small item can soon ignite aflame
burning blaze like the wooden phoenix, head
lifted high into blackened sky, ash flakes like snow
the lighter invigorates in you that old feeling,
smothered desires to become the flaming bird,
to lift yourself into an endless night. to burn.
his lighter gleams a winking eye, chanting in veins
a throb of deep craving devotion, fingers itch
to clutch inside your palm. swirling snakes
            entwined,
forked tongues flicker to taste, absorb and
dominate your flowering aroma. a tiny budding rose
constricted among starlit scales; petals weeping.
woman's face engraved on smooth surface
nose buried in rose's delicate embrace, snakes
become flowing hair, wrapped around svelte neck

when you grasp it, the metal burns. thrums
the rhythm of your heart echoes inside.
this lighter is your destiny, beckoning. you know
what you must do. you know what you must burn.
take what isn't yours and hide away in warmth,
splay spider limbs across an ocean of blankets
imagine the wizard here, looming atop your nudity
spread legs to reveal sacred space, slip inside
this found keepsake, private delicacy
like wizard's thick finger, open wide this
cavern of skin spread over sting of metal —
becomes part of you; he will never know.
the wizard will never discover
                          this buried treasure.
he will never recognize these deep desires
or attempt to seek what you have found.
ecstasy hot and sharp flickers like the snakes
licking your insides. you are one with the flame
how you've always dreamed to be.

Prometheus Butane Blues

THE WIZARD

Way back when
before tweets crawled out of time's digital soup onto brainy shore
before they grew arms & legs
before they were able to carry our secret thoughts swiftly into every heart
causing damnation sometimes, validation other times
before there were tweets, there were twinkles in the sky
sometimes those twinkles would spit fire & that'd be the only fire we'd get
back then, gods & goddesses were tweets that'd happen randomly
they'd burst through the dark & make you go crazy
maybe if you were lucky, they'd hand you a fireball so you could light up '
your cigarette
back then, we didn't have access to fire, no candles with heart to make
bored lovers sweat
back then, humanity wandered aimlessly from cave to cave
unlit blunts in their hands
we couldn't get high, people in the sky had to say yes, so we were always
losing our minds
playing dodgeball with dino skulls & praying for a release, shadowboxing in badlands
but you can't see bruises without any glow, no such thing as pain
if your brain doesn't flow

then one day, this god named Prometheus took pity on humanity
he stood atop a mountain and declared, "They need their vanity"
so he staged a one-god heist to steal some divine fire from impossible heaven
no one to drive the getaway car, no one to play lookout, but it was all cool
Prometheus successfully broke into the vaulted ashtray & stole first-degree burns
he delivered them to tribes of depression and declared, "Now you can smoke up"
then everybody got high, started talking about their dreams
vagueposting on cave walls
music bloomed from the ash, but then Prometheus was punished
gods chained him to a rock
everyday this annoying bird would peck at his liver until it was gone
then it would grow back
the pain would begin again, but it was worth it
because now humanity could get high too
it's really a heartwarming tale, a god sacrificing his divinity so people could tell stories
could sit around a campfire playing guitars made of swamp skin

& singing terrible songs
at least now they possessed the glow, at least now they could color in their thoughts
at least now they could sign their names in the sand & watch the water
lay identities to waste
at least now they had sharp shine to cut open the future, finally free
when the cold's erased

Promethean fire gave birth to all sorts of new & younger fires
but the original ball of flame
Prometheus brought down from space still kinda exists today
the heat was deconstructed
into a river of butane that was eventually used to fill cheap plastic lighters
to sell at bodegas
but not your typical bodega, but a magical one that travels the globe
on a cloud of hookah smoke
it randomly appears in a city that really needs it, full of bruised people
who're down & out
who're addicted to everything, so that when the bodega appears
people think, "What is this?"
then they go in & the prices are so good they buy all the cigarettes
all the Promethean lighters
then they go outside in the moonlight, maybe in the overcast rooflight,
& when they light up
it's the strangest feeling, they feel like they're finally free
not because of what they're smoking
but what they used to light it up
that Promethean promise of all the glow in the world
that with a little bit of luck & a lot of blind faith, you can steal the shine from heaven
that you can be heavy with glow too, the magical bodega
never appears in the same place twice
& if you're fortunate to fall into one you can only buy one lighter, but it'll never die
if you throw it against a wall it won't explode, you'll have it your whole life
it's my most prized possession, the ability to channel all your inner fire
to wear as armor your truest self-expression

Dita

THE DOLL

Eleven years of ballet, rond de jambes,
relevéz, French vocabulary memorized
your lack of length first stultifies — then bomb
of breasts a childhood dream pulverized.

In vintage lingerie, midnight chassé
apartment twirls, pink kitchen chaînes.
Daydreaming layered tulle, piano days,
you stage design yourself a naked way.

You use your curves, 1940's sass. Strip
with port de bras, bespoke pliés for cash.
In ballet peach pancake tutu, crimson lip,
you rush to arabesque in neon lights. Flash

a thong, pointe-shoed topless pirouette,
a domination classical, vedette.

I, Doll

THE DOLL

was idolatry — pretending to be
dependent, idle twirling womanchild,
chaînés to wolves, wizards. A pretty please,
diseased, undressed, digested & defiled,

the bleeding smile, sutures, eyelashes match
a Mary Magdalene chiffon bequest
unbuttoned lace Lolita dress, years stashed
pink tissue paper, cedar chest — no guess

at size because you redesigned me small
to dance — romance, happenstance removed.
I wait until your exit, let them fall —
dress, vestiges of you but black pointe shoes—

the trappings of a life I lived as doll.
I dance in nothing, night, and I am all.

Firefly

The Firebird is Born

THE FIREBIRD

the flicker of a single flame before your eyes
mystifies, you want to allow it to consume,
lick its furious tongue; unsatisfied, parched -
yearning for fuel. what will you allow it to take
from you? – this fever of passion & ripeness
tucked tightly between your thighs, metallic
           sunrise   glinting.

this flicker of golden light in your eye transports
to an earlier time, strike of sulfur, flame upon your
fingers twirling like a dancer, hips flaring out and
enchanting you - your mother rests upstairs
after sending you to your room without dinner
punishment for sliding down the banister
pretending to be a dancer just like the flames
and leaping from the bottom to soar like the Firebird
telling her, I want to be the flames, and the look of
fear, terror sharp & thick before sending you away
only for you to sneak downstairs unbidden, dead
of blackest night. flick of flame, it crackles -
strike into brilliance, click the lighter to life, birth.
violent the way it eagerly licks and begs for more.

there is no thought in this action of yours,
no hostility. you do not intend to destroy, you just
want to become the flames. you want to give them
the fuel they so desire. like a burning between
your thighs, a fire rising through your body. you want
to set it free. the flickering flame held between
two fingers, a clutch and then a drop - careless,
thoughtless. it breeds creation. becomes a burning
ember in the middle of the world, creates a core

and here is where you feel you can spread your arms
prickled now with feathers, blossoming to the surface
a rose that has yet to unfurl its petals but slowly
begins to be. a blooming seed spreading its leaves
after the deep winter frost, shaking off the cold.
there is no cold here, as the flames begin to devour
their way through the wood, crackling and sparking
as they   start to   burn.

open the front door and spin across the midnight lawn
watch as the house you have grown in becomes
an ember, shining through darkness. glimmering
and glinting like an eye that winks. the wintry air
like a cloak, pimples of goose flesh across arms,
pricking at bare legs. lace fluttering at your knees
silk nightgown shimmering in the moonlight, a flame
in yourself and shining across the snow-crossed grass
heat begins to flicker into the night, caressing and
lingering like strong fingers, stroking across your back
all along the length of you. as if you have become a
firefly, flickering there and rising from the grass to
spread your light, show the world just how brightly
you plan to ignite. you are tiny, insignificant, but
you shine. as your world crumbles before you,
everything you have known gone in the ashes
childish dreams and disasters, your own mother
perished from the smoke, they said, she didn't wake.
she couldn't bear to see what you had become.

the Firebird is born within, and you must now continue
burning from your very core, cradling the colored embers
within the dark cavern which used to house your
            beating   heart.

American Fire Doll

THE DOLL

Midnight door creaks means hide your head. Shut eyes.
Hold breath. Feign sleep. Play dead. Some nights, he peeks;
pulls covers to your knees. Tonight's surprise —
blue eyes he leaves, smoke, butterscotch scent, treat

he keeps inside his pick-up truck. "Fire doll" —
he shakes you, lifts her up in your twill sheets,
buttercup, singed nightgown, wool blanket shawl,
his bedtime story two girls recall, speech

about this one, who's real as you, pulled from
tall blaze, small rescue. "She's lost her home;
she'll spend the night." Another unwelcome
silhouette backlit, firefly nightlight comes

this strange little flame to sleep beside you stokes
blue iris flickers. Your lungs fill with smoke.

Downfall

THE FIREBIRD

begin to constantly wear your disguise
crown of thorns dipped in red, dangling

above your head. no trace of purity or
sacrifice. your name will only be shunned
woven together with life's thread but happier

— apart — and every time you try to achieve
the past slips through fingers like ribbons,
ribbons of water attached to a chemise

locked in infinite pirouettes, strings
constantly unraveling & shimmering in
fading light, after all

stars always burn brightest
before they implode.

The Last Enchantment

THE DOLL

The truth is telescopic when he's tall —
some distant, obfuscated wrinkled star,
uncollimated features, bone casket pall,
intentions blurred beneath a visage, far,

whose tears invade reposing dolls. You choke,
soaked damask sofa — sadness, waterfall.
First-time-believing, near death, a dream, deepthroat,
doomed floater, saline, screams, piano shawl

around breasts, buttermilk — his drips, despair,
your burnout silk. His desolation, your
destruction, swallowing 'til fireflies, bear
him shrunken, wallowing, weak, to dollhouse door.

His last enchantment spent becoming small,
through true love's tiny threshold, he must crawl.

Death and The Firefly

THE DOLL

One dies, side-eyed, surprised. Survives pine jamb
collision long enough to realize,
it's now sidewise, seizing by an old man,
a plastic portico.   His swarm, he spies,
retreating constellation from table top
abandons insect, human dropped — same guy
who summoned, cracked window, shrinking thoughts
until he's caught by countless claws. Flies,
with compound eyes, community of wings,
the one at elbow gleams until its crash,
a strobe light on the floor. Everything
is waiting to let go. One final thrash
into a darkness, snuffing out the pride.
Was his whole life to get this man inside?

A Dollhouse Mausoleum in a Forest of Scalpels

THE WIZARD

People used to say that witches were switchblades wearing black dresses
that when they danced, new wind would burst from old tombs
hurricanes of quilted wounds, a shift in the scent of freedom
a deletion of knights and the freeing of damsels, people are afraid of change
cutting yourself up into little pieces until each part beats with its own heart
then history happens, the proliferation of time, churches became cafes
then cafes do enough drugs, earn their sea legs, and transform into clubs
then there are drinks that make you swim to the bottom, too much youth
and you're left with nothing but ghouls, angels with no conscience
and demons who lose their names because of science, too much of a tragedy
so you knock out all your teeth, go to the dentist, and call it comedy

people used to say that Marx was born in a manger
that the hammer was a cross in the desert
now there are entrepreneurs who clone themselves and celebrate with a party
they talk about what needs to change and since they all agree
they prick their fingers until they bleed, shake hands, and declare
"Now we're a corporation"
then they shape nations, harvest hives, and murder all the ghosts
who led interesting lives
at some point, we started suffering from the curse of bigness
skyscrapers hiding under our beds stabbing skyward and piercing through our pillows
so that when we dream, we only dream of falling, falling into
something smaller than ourselves
back to the time when people would say, "It's the little things"
back to the time when we would dance and it meant something

sometimes I look at my reflection and remember
when all of earth was a fingertip away
in a dream we didn't know how to dream, but we kept dreaming anyways
sometimes I tell myself that our biggest sin is forgetting how to cry
when a storm blows clothes onto naked footprints in the snow
because what footprints want is to be unencumbered
to be one with the shine, belonging to the bite
our feet, our legs, have minds of their own, and desperately want rhythm again
it is their antidepressant, their drug, they want nothing to do

with the rest of our skeleton
then bigness happened and that bigness gave birth to stillness
and that stillness enjoys dressing up in sadness
and none of us know what to do anymore
people used to say, "Young America swings the world"
people would dance and governments would collapse, a bit of soul
and we all had heart attacks

maybe this is my suicide note, the horoscopic ramblings of a wizard
stricken with dementia
I worry I've become a creep, a predator, that time has turned my eyes
into a couple of sharks
abuse led to magic and magic gave me the world, but now everything's backwards
oh dyslexia
smartphones made from the severed tongues of poets, surgeons tripping balls
in national parks
taking scalpels to redwoods and removing their hearts, then the surgeons
turn the scalpels inward
remove their own human hearts and fill the emptiness with tree hearts
suddenly their bodies
branch out in different directions, then they put their human hearts in the tree holes
then the trees get real sad, because they're more human, then they get angry
lots of rage
then they want to conquer the forest and then the sea
and then they dream of the sky and stars
the world is upside down, airplanes made from the severed legs of dancers
who had it all
airports where the Starbucks puts cyanide in the Frappuccino
where brain freeze is permanent

and I still imagine a world where every road trip leads to Swan Lake, a lake of tears
sorcerers on their deathbeds turning everyone into birds
sadness turning into happiness
everyone who has been beaten down flying towards the sun
and slicing off pieces of fire
back on earth, they poke holes in their own bodies and shove in all the heat
all the burning
over time, our warmest desires evolve into fireflies that fly around inside our bodies
every person is just a frequency of fireflies uniting together for a common good
to love, to touch, to make an impact and that's why our eyes sparkle sometimes
my sparkle, it seems, is fading into the night and I'm losing my mind
thinking I could shrink the world into the palm of my hand and make it better

thinking I could shrink a dancer into a doll and make her magic shine brighter
thinking birds could bloom in basements
thinking attic air wouldn't make them go mad

when did I become the creeper in the bushes, the tyrant in the castle
the dictator at the podium
when did I become what needs to be put in a museum, what needs to be dethroned
and executed
when did I become more hashtag than star, more noise than symphony
all-consuming toxicity
when did that orphan born in the dirt with plastic bags and Red Bull bones become an
asshole
when did he become a puppet master pulling strings, a deity clouding over
a little dollhouse
then he starts crying for what he has turned into, his tears flooding
the Victorian floorboards
blowing out the little lamps, the doll almost drowns, and there's this knife-sharpening
revelation
now we have become corporations of melancholy and unfulfillment
bigness swallowing all
so I decide I must cut myself into tiny pieces, gouge into me, and perform
one last spell
I wanted to end up better than this, but here we go, the dollhouse will be
my final resting place
maybe a dance with the dancer I shrank, apologize, do what I can to make her
big again

one cut leads to several cuts and before long fireflies are flying out
of my withered body
youth peels off flake by flake like an avalanche and then I'm an abominable shell
of a man
a crushed can of the worst beer rolling in the wind like it all means nothing
in the recyclable end
then there's the shadow of a giant firebird flying overhead because the roof is gone
only stars
then the buzzing of the bugs busting out of my bones, trails of fire as they lift me
off the ground
then I'm floating like a rock star during the last concert of their life
and the crowd's going crazy
a parade of firefly pallbearers carrying me to my death or maybe my resurrection
there's music
a history of magic passes before my eyes, cauldron after cauldron

off a greasy conveyor belt
they shatter somehow, but everything is bottomless, so they crash
and then there's confetti
eyelashes floating straight up in the air like an optometrist rapture
and then everything's blurry
then I'm carried across the threshold where I collapse
and then I see the dancer approaching

Corpse, Cannibal

THE DOLL

Love crawls to grandfather clock, winding down,
small sitting room cadaver, found, who fell
from slither, sunken chest. Beside him, ground,
detecting weakest breaths, you notice smells

inhuman rot, that dying firefly, whom
you forgot, death rattles, wings, wee front porch.
Head wound free bleeds its white viscous doom,
abdomen glows remnants, defueled blowtorch

whose light was magic without scorch — cool, tool.
A golden rule stays shaking hands. True love
can still fail biology in high school.
Its intended, dying, eyes you above —

will whisper, "this time — kind you must dissect;
corpse, cannibal, this creature you protect."

Love Could Be a Plastic Knife

THE DOLL

you'll wield one night to save a life. Removes
wing covers languidly, veined cellophane,
its grey-winged mystery. Excision proves
your love for him, this wizard, captor, bane
then friend who nearly drowned you with his tears,
diminished you to ease his fears. Yet you
dissect insects for him, yellow glimmers,
reveal of abdomen. Magnified through
his magic, half your size, bent antennae,
black bandit pointillistic eyes. White ooze,
you'll use, bug body parts, burnt sienna
pulverized arthropod hearts with pointe shoes.
Bioluminescence could save his life
the way that love could be a plastic knife.

On Your Deathbed, You Will Throw up All the Places You've Called Home

THE WIZARD

They say that smells trigger such vivid memories and I often imagine the brain
as this cotton candy desert of noses, trillions of them slowly crawling like turtles
under the blazing hot sun of memory, beams of regret setting hairs on fire
then the sun gives way to an icy cool moon, nighttime freezing puddles of snot
so you're always slipping on your saddest memories & I feel that in the afterlife
you're like a janitor or groundskeeper wandering through the fragments
of your expired life
shoveling all these non-functioning noses into a landfill of senseless amnesia
all the smells you hold dear or all the smells you fear fading away
forever & ever
what good are memories if they need all these other things to blister into realization
memory sits on the shoulders of a giant, but that giant is drunk, an addict
and he wants to die

but smell never really did it for me, it's better when flowers grow out of your tongue

before death almost sweeps me off my feet, a comet-bright dancer is feeding me firefly
powder
jamming spoonfuls down my throat like an aggressive assembly line
the factory of my rebirth
tastes awful, white blood tasting like rain from a hungover cloud that only eats
cancerous planes
I don't know why she's bathing me with resurrection, I want punishment...
not another chance
I'm vomiting too, but it's not mucky liquid or chunks of agriculture
I'm vomiting little cities
all the cities I've ever called home, there are warzones
where the breakfast is bombs benedict
there are renaissances where castles rise from floorboards
& spray everyone with champagne
I'm spitting out bricks of taverns where the best minds of terminated generations
dreamt big
they found love in the bare shoulders of jukeboxes, in the broken windows of orgies
and art
then they started revolutions that monster-trucked over inequality
but eventually ran out of gas

but momentum never lasts long, you gotta dig deep & hope your brain outlasts
your bones

people like me should be dead & buried, men like me shouldn't have lasted this long
a kingdom of uninspired madness that grows & grows, but nobody wants to touch it
so the kingdom gets mad, goes crazy, sharpens its crown of thorns & runs headfirst into
the sky
so the sky punctures open & these tired angels fall through the holes
& hit the machined ground
so the tired, bruised angels stand up & dust themselves off & look around
they get sick
so the angry angels refuse to perform miracles, so they wander around
spreading bitterness
so the motormouthed angels talk about heaven, how they long to penetrate
those gates again
it's a disgrace, a kingdom that shreds off our skins & replaces our armor
with something sadder
yet the dancer shrunken by a tyrannical universe of suits & psychotherapists
touches my lips
she traces the wrinkles of my tomb with her graceful toes & redraws my maps
with her roads

but in death, genuine intimacy is easier to hold...
in life, maybe your breaths get in the way

Cleansing

THE FIREBIRD

a firefly visits you // blinking light that appears
like a hallucination. you have no time to realize
it should not be here // you are already captivated //
possessed by its brilliance after months of seeing nothing,
nothing // but your mermaid friend who lives in
the wall of the basement, stolen bit of ocean and saltwater
she breathes through gills // enchants you
with a single verse // melodic spells she inherited from the
Wizard. this firefly visitor seems so familiar
like an old friend or someone you've known for a while
not a smell exactly // just a feeling that you know
who has entered as a temporary light // beaming golden light.
the presence of the Wizard is weakened tonight
you follow the firefly up the stairs // it bobs and spins
wings // captured on invisible wind // lifting up
through the air and beckoning you to follow along // follow
into the dead of night // the unknown // the
dwelling of the Wizard // this mysterious castle which you
have explored only once before // the hidden
secret of the lighter // still bright between your legs // tucked
away // in your womanhood like a promise
a whisper of destruction // somehow you know exactly
all the damage // a single flick of a lighter
can cause // in no more than an instant // in no more than
a moment // opened in a lapse of time // forgotten
but never forgiven // you the sole survivor of that first fire
burning brilliant // in the sight of the lawn
burning away all the frost // and your tears like diamonds
frozen on your cheeks. // this is what propels
you forward // what motivates your feet to continue // after,
after you have bid your // farewells to those
you thought you once loved // who deserve no more to glisten
beyond you // always shining brighter // always
threatening // to overcome your light // with their own burning
ball of glitter. // this will not be allowed
you think as you // reach up the stairs // throw open the door
leading down // to your imprisonment // down
into your depths // smell of soil where you have discovered

your soul // the neglected Firebird // feels close
to once again becoming free // to once again release your hold
on the monster residing inside // crying out //
the lighter // waiting to be flicked on // the flame waiting to lick
to breathe in the smoke // of its own creation
eating anything in its path // cleansing the fire-starter //
Firebird glistening in the night // dancing across the lawn
like the firefly leading you now // up the stairs // you are nothing more
than a body // all limbs // leaden // leading up
an angel without its wings // stripped // and you are now hovering
hovering above the scene // watching as you go
destructive bomb // flare flaming up just about to reach
your core // a fuse ticking away // time slipping
feet move below you like a robot // automaton moving
without thought // moving beyond obstacles
with ease // finding finally moon-drenched room //
full of flickering lights // full of fireflies glinting
final dance beneath a full moon // glowing inside the sashes
drenching across // the Firebird's naked skin
like that silken nightdress // lacing across your knees, tracing ankles.
allowing you to dance again // kicking up dust
in your path // just the ashes // ashes within which you will rise //
                    you all will.
the lighter hidden away // a flicker of fire in your belly.
you won't use it until you're sure // until you see what you intend to burn
once you look inside your enemy's eyes // unveil
the true meaning behind your intent // why you wish to destroy this, too.
just as you will always wonder // why you could no longer
live in a world that included your mother // why you had to
become the firefly which // morphed into Firebird.
it was always fire which would grant you // freedom you sought.
sacred bathing // cleansing
of your sins and soul.

Torch

Anatomy is Alchemy

THE DOLL

The body is a spell. Ten fingertips,
magicians, disrobe their damoiselle — slow,
while he is sitting, puppy, restless, nips
at black pointe shoes. Your finger tells him no.

Obedience he'll choose. He won't require
a potion. Vertebrae compel. Observe
over shoulder, stoic but his tell: two fires
that smolder inside pupils. Heat he deserves

for shrinking — even thinking you are small.
Your body is enchantment he didn't see
at all. You indicate the floor. He crawls
towards a doll vibrating sorcery,

below rotating, naked piqué turns.
Each kiss, even a pointe shoe, he will earn.

It's the Tenderness that Kills You

THE WIZARD

Intimacy is an execution, the touch of lightning bolts
disrobing your sense of self, someone else's breathing
turning your campfire stories into buzzworthy obituaries
everything you thought you knew becoming trash

and you hate yourself for it, the undeclaration of your independence
the worst parts of yourself posing for the camera, shaky hands
digging into your chest and pulling out your heart, but it's not really your heart
just another camera, all the magic in the world can't hide the truth

you're an illusion, all these years thinking you're larger than life
that you alone possess the secret of joy, a flick of your wrist
and balled-up tissues on bedroom floors bloom into flowers
but they're not really flowers, just antidepressants playing dress-up

now you're being touched and it's making you feel small and subservient
this is how it should be, kissing the scarred feet of those who'll inherit the world

It Makes You Feel Better for a Moment

THE DOLL

to see him drop, reducible, his lips
embracing box of black satin, pointe shoe.
It's lonely, too, not you — performance
without the benefit of clothes, sinewed

statue, saline demeaning both of you
until you, leaning, offer him your hand. To brush
away these tears, he has to stand, subdued
only by love tempering an ancient lust.

He carries you up walnut stairs, inside
crimson canopy, chestnut curls, that fall
with flesh, upon a cream bedspread. Astride
he finds what's nested, unmolested, small.

Beneath his body, first time, you will know
love catches you finally letting go.

Destined for Doom

THE FIREBIRD

Gaze upon the woman in fiery light —
tiny doll, glowing. she floats with fireflies
straddled by the Wizard, in his clutches
this tiny one you've tried to protect; failed.
now she is consumed like an ocean wave
fumbling, crashing down and shattering
into a million edges. she shines like magic,
shimmering gold. despite her ragged beauty,
she is unable to be saved. destined for doom.
you must save her the way you saved your
mother, those years ago. bring flames to lick
her skin, consume her limbs. release your
clutch upon enchanted lighter. flick of finger
ignites trembling blaze. mold this burning
light with cedar dollhouse frame. wildfire,
Victorian embers it will become, devouring
the living doll and her wizardly captor
in a gulf of blistering combustion.
crimson bed frame curtains ignite,
become a burning grave.

Torch

THE DOLL

When he's inside you they will glow, fireflies
illuminating freckled skin within,
aflutter, nervous system oxidized
lost, lidless eyes coated, hemoglobin,

careening toward abdomen, a nest
abreast blue veins, viscera. Bless with light
bleak blight, this temporality, your chest
fluorescing, rest of you radiating bright

pink, warm between him, his progeny swarm,
incubating wings — hypodermis clings.
Flesh, incandescent, magic has transformed
eclipses blaze, the heat, haze, surrounding —

Your world in smoke unseen until the scorch,
occupied inside, you become his torch.

Extinguish

THE WIZARD

I'm standing on the beach with my ghost beside me
we think we're watching whales wash ashore, but they're not whales
they're mammalian jukeboxes from the 1950s
a coin-operated Cold War from when the world was supposed to end
their cords are plugged into nothing, but they're still spitting out songs
the best songs about fire, flames, or things burning
is this what it looks like when you lose passion over time?
when the fire inside you has no place to go, but you keep singing anyway

We see the glow of fire in the distance and a haunting of shadows
my ghost whispers, "I don't know why firefighters exist
you can't run from momentum, you can't fight it
when love goes up in flames, it's not the heart that smells rotten... but the sky itself
raindrops that feel like a dead man's fingers on the back of your neck
we're always ready for a fresh new start
surgeons made from ash dissecting old anatomy
so we might walk in newness of life"

I don't know when my ghost started quoting the Bible
when he started cutting the cocaine of optimism
with the pessimism of laundry detergent
it's a volatile mix, he's piss-poor company
but I have to remind myself that this is my future
the fire continues to spread
my ghost whispers, "Fires should die of natural causes
wouldn't it be nice if beauty leaves this world on its own terms?"

Corrosive Core

THE FIREBIRD

Small mewl comes from amidst thick smoke,
incinerating dollhouse emits flumes - blackened, charred
the way you imagine your heart — you only wanted to save her.
Pathetic cries come from a cornered room, reach in
smell the singe of burnt hair, skin of your arm sizzles
remove in your palm a miniature, paper-crafted kitten
origami mystery with hint of magic, enchantments
like a real kitten, soft insistent thing inside your hand.

Wonder what you'll call this creature, innocence
created at the edge of chaos — onlooker, bystander
gawking at the wreckage, cracked spiders-web windows
fogged from heat within. desperate breath inside.
Your fingers are shaking. search for movement
        but flames consume all.

Not even the Wizard's fading magic could withstand
enchanted flame from his cherished lighter, the doll
brought him to his end.

your fingers are shaking. charred kitten starts purring

/// *shattering windows like feathers molting* ///

these images will form inside you, you'll never forget
as you watch the destruction,

        corrosive core,

           dollhouse eaten from within.

Heart Shaped Heap, Gray Ash

THE DOLL

Beach castle sans a single grain of sand —
walls, caul, dollhouse creation, decrepit
runed man, last flourish of his palsied hand,
human diminishment without regret

until beneath youth's mask, he lets her see
a frailty of centuries, his cruel
destruction, hundreds just like her with pleas
turned peeps — enchanted birds made minuscule.

Her own, last doll, wet gurgled, tears, death wish
she swallowed decades, fears then offered him
a resting place, their fingers twine, legs twist
about his waist. Flames amalgamate them.

Beach castle disappears, the sandless hill;
their heart-shaped heap, gray ashes, never will.

End.

Acknowledgments

We want to thank everyone for reading and for your invaluable support. Thank you for taking the time to join us in our dark fantasy opera.

Special thanks to those who published versions of these poems:

Angelical Ravings Zine, APEP Publications, Awkward Mermaid, Boston Accent Lit, The Cabinet of Heed, Chantarelle's Notebook, Constellate Literary Journal, Dear Reader: Poetry, Déraciné, Dusk & Shiver, Feminine Collective, The Ginger Collect, Instant, A Literary Magazine, {isacoustic}, Marías at Sampaguitas, Menacing Hedge, Mojave He[art] Review, Mookychick, Moonchild Magazine, Neologism Poetry Journal, Neon Mariposa, New Mexico Review, Rhythm of the Bones: Dark Marrow, Selcouth Station Press, South Broadway Ghost Society, SWWIM, Three Drops from a Cauldron, Twist in Time Literary Magazine, Vamp Cat Magazine.*

The Characters and the Poets Who Wrote Them

Kristin Garth (THE DOLL): THE DOLL like the poet who writes her, Kristin Garth, is captivated with dollhouses. In this story *A Victorian Dollhousing Ceremony*, THE DOLL lives inside both a mundane and magical society where wizards are whispers you might wander into one night. THE DOLL certainly does, after a lifetime of tragic encounters with men, she meets a wizard at a party, drinks a concoction and winds up inside a dollhouse. It all happens in much the same way as the poet, Kristin Garth, took a sleeping pill one night and ended up in a nightmare about being dollhoused that turned into a sonnet that turned into a talk with Justin Karcher and then Tianna G. Hansen that turned into the book which you now hold in your hands. It's one of ten books by Kristin Garth you can read about (and order annotated and signed copies) at her website (kristingarth.com).

Tianna G. Hansen (THE FIREBIRD): Tianna has been writing her whole life. Her debut poetry collection *Undone, Still Whole* was released from APEP Publications in May. This is her second book and her first collaboration. Playing the role of THE FIREBIRD meant taking on a role of liberation and release. THE FIREBIRD began as a woman/dancer who always tried to please men, who craved the attention and approval of her body image and as a person. She must learn to accept her own love and appreciation, take back her control and power in her life while battling with her fatal envy of the one woman who seems to succeed over everything in her life, THE DOLL. Find more of Tianna's writing at CreativeTianna.com, follow her on Twitter @tiannag92 / FB @tiannaghansen / IG @tgghansen24.

Justin Karcher (THE WIZARD): Justin Karcher is a Pushcart-nominated poet and playwright born and raised in Buffalo, New York. Breathing life into THE WIZARD, the book's villain (or anti-hero), was an exhilarating and humbling experience for him. He is the author of several books, including *Tailgating at the Gates of Hell* (Ghost City Press, 2015). He is also the editor of *Ghost City Review* and co-editor of the anthology *My Next Heart: New Buffalo Poetry* (BlazeVOX [books], 2017). He tweets @Justin_Karcher.

Russ Daum (the illustrator) often draws in the midst of chaos and lets his subconscious guide his hand in seeking a calm spirit. You can find out out more about him at scrawlsscratchesscribbles.home.blog and on twitter at Tranquility Base @RussDaum.

Rhythm & Bones Press (the publisher) is a small independent press from Pennsylvania dedicated to highlighting dynamic and inspirational authors whose work deserves to be acknowledged. They specialize in authors who write with personal emotion and those with trauma to portray to the world. They aim to help turn Trauma into Art. Visit them at rhythmnbone.com for more information, to find more of their books, or to check out their online literary magazine and Necropolis blog. This is their first published collaboration. Find them on Twitter @RhythmBonesLit, on Instagram @RhythmBonesPress, and on Facebook @RhythmBonesPress. A new anthology is upcoming, based around astrology, co-edited by Tianna G. Hansen and Kristin Garth, titled *Defy Your* Stars. They are also opening submissions for a new venture this October 2019, called BoneChaps, where they will select chapbooks for publication in 2020. Be sure to follow them on GoodReads.

More by Rhythm & Bones Press

You Are Not Your Rape anthology
(December 2018)

Lady Saturn – Wanda Deglane
(February 2019)

Puritan U – Kristin Garth
(March 2019)

The saint of milk and flames – Kate Garrett
(April 2019)

Flowers of the Flesh – Effy Winter
(May 2019)

Coming Soon

The Discontinuity at the Waistline – Marion Deutsche Cohen
(July 2019)

*Was it R*pe* – Elisabeth Horan
(August 2019)

at the water's edge – Nadia Gerassimenko
(September 2019)

CPSIA information can be obtained
at www.ICGtesting.com
Printed in the USA
BVHW040600090819
555377BV00004B/30/P